On every continent and nearly every country around the world God-called men and women are being equipped in seminaries to go and make disciples, followers of Jesus. These ministers are tasked with the responsibility of transformative ministry. Alemseged Alemu raises a compelling question, "Are these ministers experiencing a transformative learning experience *themselves* during their theological training?" Dr. Alemu, a dean and professor himself, has designed a robust research framework to answer this question by surveying and interviewing both graduates and faculty in five theological institutions in Ethiopia. His findings are powerful and can be transferred from professors to students to congregations. Reading this book can be your first step to transforming your classroom and your ministry.

Ken Coley, EdD
Senior Professor of Christian Education,
Director of EdD studies,
Southeastern Baptist Theological Seminary, North Carolina, USA

In this ground-breaking study of Ethiopian ministry education, Dr. Alemseged K. Alemu examines factors related to transformative change in students enrolled in five Evangelical seminaries. His findings are both encouraging and enlightening. A majority of students report their seminary experience is broadly transformative, but there is much that seminaries and their faculties could do to better equip graduates as agents of transformative change in the congregations they serve and the communities their congregations impact. While the focus of this research is limited to Ethiopian seminaries, other ministry trainers will have no difficulty in finding implications for their contexts as well.

Robert W. Ferris, PhD
Professor Emeritus,
Columbia International University, South Carolina, USA

Transformation and transformative learning have become household terms in higher education. These buzz words have appeared in institutional manifestos as beacons for quality higher education even though, for many, transformation remains elusive. In this outstanding research, Dr. Alemu has connected transformative learning not only to our teaching methodologies but also to the critical relationships that exist between teachers and students, as typified in the relationship between Christ and his disciples. The research conclusion that relational instructional strategies can enhance transformative learning provides critical insights for teachers and learners who engage with educational ventures toward transformation. The research provides credible data, interpretations, and recommendations that every teacher pursuing transformational outcomes for their students must read and engage with. This work is highly recommended for Christian institutions of higher learning whose mandate is to form Christ-like leaders for the church.

John Jusu, PhD
Regional Director for Anglophone Africa, Overseas Council

The goal of any theological education should be to produce transformed graduates who can bring a visible impact by transforming the church and society in their respective contexts. But the transformation of the church and society is highly dependent on having graduates who have experienced transformation themselves, while they are in theological institutions. In *Predictive Factors for Transformative Learning within ACTEA Related Theological Institutions*, Alemseged K. Alemu presents for us the non-negotiable factors necessary to see transformative learning in higher theological institutions. These predictive factors – that result in transformative learning – are born both from empirical research and the many years of personal experience the writer has as an academic leader in Ethiopia. The book can serve as a guide for theological school leaders and faculty members to be very intentional in delivering transformative learning that will produce theologically transformed graduates. I highly encourage all who are involved in theological education, in one way or another, to make use of this valuable resource as they labor to produce transformed graduates for God's kingdom work.

Frew Tamrat, PhD
Principal,
Evangelical Theological College, Addis Ababa, Ethiopia

Predictive Factors for Transformative Learning within ACTEA-Related Theological Institutions in Ethiopia

Alemseged K. Alemu

MONOGRAPHS

© 2022 Alemseged K. Alemu

Published 2022 by Langham Monographs
An imprint of Langham Publishing
www.langhampublishing.org

Langham Publishing and its imprints are a ministry of Langham Partnership

Langham Partnership
PO Box 296, Carlisle, Cumbria, CA3 9WZ, UK
www.langham.org

ISBNs:
978-1-83973-208-9 Print
978-1-83973-621-6 ePub
978-1-83973-622-3 Mobi
978-1-83973-623-0 PDF

Alemseged K. Alemu has asserted his right under the Copyright, Designs and Patents Act, 1988 to be identified as the Author of this work.

All rights reserved. No part of this publication may be reproduced, stored in a retrieval system or transmitted, in any form or by any means, electronic, mechanical, photocopying, recording or otherwise, without the prior written permission of the publisher or the Copyright Licensing Agency.

Requests to reuse content from Langham Publishing are processed through PLSclear. Please visit www.plsclear.com to complete your request.

Scripture quotations are from The Holy Bible, English Standard Version® (ESV®), copyright © 2001 by Crossway, a publishing ministry of Good News Publishers. Used by permission. All rights reserved.

Scripture quotations marked (NIV) are taken from the Holy Bible, New International Version®, NIV®. Copyright © 1973, 1978, 1984, 2011 by Biblica, Inc.™ Used by permission of Zondervan.

British Library Cataloguing-in-Publication Data
A catalogue record for this book is available from the British Library

ISBN: 978-1-83973-208-9

Cover & Book Design: projectluz.com

Langham Partnership actively supports theological dialogue and an author's right to publish but does not necessarily endorse the views and opinions set forth here or in works referenced within this publication, nor can we guarantee technical and grammatical correctness. Langham Partnership does not accept any responsibility or liability to persons or property as a consequence of the reading, use or interpretation of its published content.

For my family.

Every good and perfect gift comes from the Father above! (James 1:17)

Contents

Acknowledgments xiii

Abstract xv

Abbreviations xvii

Chapter 1 1
The Problem and Its Setting
    Introduction 1
    Statement of the Problem 5
    Research Purpose 6
    Background of the Colleges Included in the Study 6
        Shiloh Bible College Ethiopia 7
        Ethiopian Full Gospel Theological Seminary 7
        Meserete Kristos College 8
        Mekane Yesus Seminary 8
        Evangelical Theological College 9
    Research Questions and Hypotheses 9
    Limitations and Delimitations of the Study 10
    Definition of Terms 11
    Research Assumptions 13
    Summary of the Research Process 13
    Significance of the Study 14

Chapter 2 17
Literature Review
    Introduction 17
    Theological Foundations for Transformative Learning 17
        Transformation – the Purpose of Theological Education 20
        The Need for Graduate Transformation 21
        Biblical Understanding of Man – Foundations for
            Transformative Learning 22
        Conclusion 30
    Jack Mezirow's Transformative Learning Theory 32
        Conclusion 34
    Alternative Conceptions for Transformative Learning 35
    Transformative Learning as a Holistic Process 37
        Affective Domain 39

Cognitive Domain	42
Behavioral Domain	44
Conclusion	47
Theories of Adult Learning	49
Brain Science and Learning	49
Experiential Learning Theory – David Kolb	51
Elmer's Cycle of Learning	55
Theoretical Framework	57
Transformative Learning as a Cyclical Process	57
Transformative Learning as a Holistic Process	61
Instructional Strategies for Transformative Learning	63
Mass Instructional Strategies	68
Individualized Instructional Strategies	71
Group Instructional Strategies	74
Interpersonal Relationships in Transformative Learning	76
Chapter Summary	79
Chapter 3	**81**
Methodological Design	
Research Purpose	81
Research Questions	81
Research Methodology	82
Research Population and Sample	84
Limitation of Generalization	85
Instrumentation	86
Instrument Description	87
Validity and Reliability	88
Exploratory Factor Analysis – Transformative Learning Experience	90
Exploratory Factor Analysis – Interpersonal Relationship	93
Exploratory Factor Analysis – Instructional Strategies	94
Research Process and Data Collection	95
Chapter 4	**99**
Analysis of Findings	
Introduction	99
Presentation and Analysis of the Data	101
Research Question 1	101
Students' Perception of Transformative Learning	102
Areas of Perceived Transformation	106

  Focus Group Findings on Perceived Transformative
   Learning 107
  Contributors to Transformative Learning Experience 110
 Research Question 2 113
  Null Hypothesis 1 113
  Instructional Strategies and Frequency of Use 113
  Instructional Strategies and Influence 114
 Research Question 3 116
  Null Hypothesis 2 116
  Influence of Instructional Strategies 120
  Focus Group Findings – Instructional Strategies 123
  Explaining the Quantitative Data Using the Qualitative
   Finding 129
  Classroom Observation 130
 Research Question 4 132
  Null Hypothesis 3 132
  Student Perceptions of Influential Relationships 132
  Focus Group Findings – Interpersonal Relationships 136
 Research Question 5 139
  Null Hypothesis 4 139
  Multiple Regression Analysis with Three IVs 140
  Demographic Information 142

Chapter 5 145
Summary, Conclusion, and Recommendations
 Research Purpose 145
 Research Questions 145
 Summary of Findings 146
  Research Question 1 147
  Research Question 2 149
  Research Question 3 150
  Research Question 4 153
  Research Question 5 155
  Three-Factor Multiple Regression 155
  Relation to the Theoretical Framework 156
 Conclusions 156
  Conclusion One 157
  Conclusion Two 159
  Conclusion Three 161
  Conclusion Four 162
  Conclusion Five 162

    Applications 163
        Application One 163
        Application Two 164
        Application Three 164
        Application Four 165
        Application Five 166
        Application Six 166
        Application Seven 167
    For Further Study 167
        Recommendation One 168
        Recommendation Two 168
        Recommendation Three 168
        Recommendation Four 168
        Recommendation Five 168
        Recommendation Six 169
    Chapter Summary 169

Appendix A 171
    Survey Instrument – Students

Appendix B 179
    Focus Group Discussion Questions

Appendix C 181
    Survey Instrument – Teachers

Appendix D 185
    Original Learning Activities Survey (LAS)

Bibliography 189

List of Figures

Figure 1: A logic chain model 20

Figure 2: Cycle of transformation based on the logic chain developed by Rupen Das 31

Figure 3: Concerted functioning of the learning domains 48

Figure 4: The Lewinian experiential learning model......................................52

Figure 5: Kolb's experiential learning 55

Figure 6: Elmer's cycle of learning. 56

Figure 7: Select adult learning theories comparison chart..............................58

Figure 8: Transformative learning process (combining Mezirow, Kolb, and Elmer) 59

Figure 9: Constructs, transformative learning stages, and learning taxonomies. 61

Figure 10. Transformative learning constructs...62

Figure 11. Concerted interaction of learning domains 62

Figure 12: Variable, research question, and item correlation chart...................95

Figure 13: Transformative learning pyramid 157

Figure 14: Interactive instructional strategies for transformative learning........161

List of Tables

Table 1. Loadings of Perception of Transformative Learning Experience 90

Table 2. Subscale Inter-Correlations 93

Table 3. Factor Loadings of Interpersonal Relationships 94

Table 4. Student Survey Response Rate 100

Table 5. Teacher Survey Response Rates 101

Table 6. Focus Group Participants 101

Table 7. Student's Perception of Transformative Learning Experience 102

Table 8. Mean and Percentage of Subscales with Mean Greater Than Three 105

Table 9. Areas of Perceived Transformation 106

Table 10. Broad Categories of Perceived Areas of Change 106

Table 11. Areas of Transformation Frequency by Institution 107

Table 12. Frequency of Instructional Strategies 114

Table 13. Instructional Strategies and Their Perceived Influence 115

Table 14. Teachers' Perceptions of the Frequency of Use 117

Table 15. Comparison of the Frequency of Use 118

Table 16. Teachers Perception of the Influence of Each of the
Instructional Strategies 120

Table 17. Influence Comparison 121

Table 18. Instructional Strategies Used during Observation 130

Table 19. Student Perception of Influential Relationships 133

Table 20. Teachers' Perception of Influential Relationships 134

Table 21. Perceived Influences Due to Interpersonal Relationships 135

Table 22. Extraordinary Events Experienced 142

Table 23. Demographic Information 143

Acknowledgments

There are many people to whom I would like to express my sincere gratitude for their support, encouragement, and guidance during my study as well as the journey of writing this work. It would be impossible for me to name all, but I would like to acknowledge some. Foremost, I would like to praise God who gave me the opportunity to do my doctoral study and has provided for every need I had in order to complete that.

I would like to express my deepest gratitude to Dr. Kenneth Coley for his continuous support, care, motivation, enthusiasm, and immense knowledge during my study – without which my journey would not have gone far.

I would also like to thank my classmates for their friendship, encouragement, and prayer. My time with each of my classmates and sharing in the richness of the cultural diversity and experience each student brought into the class made my long travels to SEBTS worth it.

I am grateful to my family for their patience, love, concern, and prayers as I worked on my studies and as they had to share the responsibilities in my absence. I am especially grateful to my wife, Noo, for her love, prayer, and continued support throughout the years of my study and especially for taking her time in reading through my dissertation, commenting on my ideas and editing it for me.

I am also grateful to Ant and Eva Greenham who opened up their home and welcomed me to stay at their place for all the times I traveled to the US for my classes and who showed me incredible hospitality.

I want to thank my colleagues for sharing my responsibilities in my absence and giving me the time to complete my dissertation. I would also like to express my gratitude to Dr. Mehari Tadesse for his encouragement and guidance as I worked on the statistics part of the research. I want to thank the theological higher educational institutions that arranged for me to distribute my survey, meet with students for focus group discussions, and observe their classrooms. Their help in this process has been welcoming and I am grateful.

Finally, I would like to thank Southeastern Baptist Theological Seminary, Overseas Council International, and Serving In Mission for their support in providing me a scholarship for my studies.

Abstract

This mixed-method study examines students' perceptions of the extent they experienced transformative learning. It also examines students' perceptions of the factors that may explain the transformative learning experience they had. The students who participated in this study were graduating students from the five theological higher educational institutions in Ethiopia that have some level of accreditation with the Association of Christian Theological Education in Africa (ACTEA). For the quantitative portion of the study an adapted version of an instrument is used. There were 137 graduating students and 31 faculty members who participated in the research from all five institutions. For the qualitative portion of the study, focus group discussions and classroom observations were conducted at each of the institutions.

The findings of the study indicate that a varying number of students experienced different levels of transformative learning. It also shows that instructional strategy was a significant predictor of all four factors of transformative learning and interpersonal relationship was a significant predictor of three of the transformative learning factors. Therefore, instructional strategies that actively engage the students in their learning and close personal relationships students have with instructors and other students improve the extent students experience transformative learning.

Keywords: transformative learning, instructional strategies, theological education, relationship.

Abbreviations

LAS – Learning Activity Survey designed by Kathleen P. King
ACTEA – Association of Christian Theological Education in Ethiopia
ETC – Evangelical Theological College
SBCE– Shiloh Bible College Ethiopia
MKC – Meserete Kristos Church
MYS – Mekane Yesus Seminary
EFGBC – Ethiopian Full Gospel Bible College

CHAPTER 1

The Problem and Its Setting

Introduction

Ethiopia was under the heavy rule of the communist regime for about seventeen years (1974–1991). In its anti-Christian ideology, the communist regime forced the evangelical churches to go underground. However, as in the case of the church in the book of Acts, God was adding to the numbers of the churches. With the increase of their numbers, it became clear that the church needed to have leaders trained in the word of God to teach and shepherd the growing church. It was in response to this need that a number of the evangelical theological colleges were opened in Ethiopia.[1]

The colleges equipped men and women who provided leadership and teaching for the growing churches. Since the fall of the communist regime in 1991, the country has enjoyed the freedom of religion and the church continues to grow numerically.[2] However, the church is experiencing division and its members tend to follow individuals, as in the case of the Corinthian church (1 Cor 3:4). One evidence of this is the meeting with prime minister Abiy Ahmed on 20 June 2019, where he called together four hundred of the Ethiopian evangelical church leaders together urging them to be united and begin to work together.[3] Paul calls the church in Corinth "worldly" because they were divided, and they were not acting any different from the rest of

---

1. Evangelical Theological College, "About Us," https://etcollege.org/about-us/.
2. Mandyk, *Operation World*, 328.
3. "Abiy Ahmed Moves," Borkena.

the world. The global church is described as being spiritually impotent and that the characteristic worldview of Christians has become similar to that of their surrounding culture and "despite their professions, the lives of the vast majority of professing Christians are hardly distinguishable from those of their non-Christian neighbors."[4]

In the context where the church seems to be growing numerically but has a low impact on the society due to its division, this seminary leader is concerned why believers seem to live a life that is indistinguishable from the culture around them in spite of the number of Bible schools, colleges, and seminaries in much of the country today.

The existence of the theological educational institutions is very closely related to that of the churches. The Lausanne Movement's Cape Town Commitment states, "The mission of the church on earth is to serve the mission of God, and the mission of theological education is to strengthen and accompany the mission of the church."[5] In order for the church to serve the mission of God, it needs "faithful men and women who can guide the people of God to confront and overcome the challenges they face, and courageously and clearly fulfill their missional mandate."[6] Therefore, the foundation for the existence of theological educational institutions is to prepare men and women who are capable of guiding and empowering the church to be effective in fulfilling its mission.[7] It would then be appropriate to ask about the extent to which the theological educational institutions are equipping men and women to serve the church.

The extent to which the graduates from the theological educational institutions can contribute to the transformative ministry of the church and its impact in the world is determined by the extent to which the graduates themselves experience transformation. Dr. Perry Shaw, an adjunct professor at Arab Baptist Theological Seminary and author of *Transforming Theological Education*, explains this transformation of the graduates saying, "The goal of learning (especially as articulated in Ephesians 4) is to see men and women in community increasingly transformed into the image of Christ – and this

---

4. Ferris, Lillis, and Enlow, *Ministry Education*, 2–3.
5. Lausanne Movement, "Cape Town Commitment," II.F.4.
6. Shaw, *Transforming Theological Education*, 20.
7. Ferris, Lillis, and Enlow, *Ministry Education*; Shaw, *Transforming Theological Education*.

involves all of the cognitive, affective and behavioral dimensions."[8] It is not enough to have graduates who are informed but they must also be holistically transformed in all three domains (cognitive, affective, and behavior).

The holistic transformation of a person is the primary purpose of teaching in the Bible. Christians are commanded to be transformed in their way of life, in their attitude, and in their knowledge (Rom 12:2; 2 Tim 3:16–17; 2 Cor 3:18; 2 Tim 2:15; Ps 51:10–12, etc.). The Gospels show that Jesus taught for transformation. The story of the Samaritan woman at the well is a good illustration of this. At the end of the conversation Jesus had with the Samaritan woman, she was a different person in her personal perception of herself and her relationship with God and with others. Coley, after narrating this transformative experience of the Samaritan woman, states "We all would love to have insights into how Jesus taught so we could begin to see transformation in our group member's lives like the change demonstrated by the Samaritan woman."[9] Transformation of the learners into the likeness of the Lord Jesus Christ is the ultimate goal of any Christian teaching.

While transformation is something the Bible teaches as the goal of Christian teaching, the theory of transformative learning has become an important development in adult education since Jack Mezirow proposed it more than forty-five years ago as a phase theory whereby learners undergo a change in their perspectives. His work is primarily a rational approach to learning where the learner is engaged in critical reflection and rational discourse. Mezirow's stages for transformative learning have been embraced and used extensively for assessing and promoting transformative learning in broad contexts. The most widely used instrument for assessing possible factors for transformative learning is the one developed by Kathleen King. She used Mezirow's stages of transformative learning and developed the Learning Activities Survey (LAS), which continues to be a useful instrument in assessing factors that contribute to transformative learning in diverse contexts.

While engagement in critical reflection and participation in discourse are important aspects of learning, they alone cannot guarantee transformative learning.[10] Emotions are also significant contributors to transformative

---

8. Perry Shaw, personal email communication with researcher, 13 November 2018.
9. Coley, *Teaching for Change*, 1.
10. Cranton, *Understanding*, 96.

learning. Edward Taylor explains the role of emotions by saying, "It seems that emotions and rationality are much more interdependent than previously understood, each acting in concert with the other in the decision-making process . . . At times introspection should be de-emphasized, with greater attention and appreciation given for nonconscious ways of change."[11]

In speaking of transformative learning experiences, Dirkx in an interview with Cranton says, "such experiences have come to be called transformative experiences and are usually associated with a profound change in one's cognitive, emotional, or spiritual way of being."[12] Therefore, transformative learning is not limited to the cognitive process of learning, but it is also a result of other dimensions of learning such as a person's affect and behavior working in concert with each other.[13]

Theological educational institutions should seek for students to have a transformative learning experience that makes a difference in their ministry both in the church and in society. Among many other possible factors for creating an environment for transformative learning, the instructional strategies used within the institutions and the diverse interpersonal relationships must be evaluated.

In order to determine the impact of the different learning experiences in bringing about transformation, a theological institution may need to determine two things: first, do the students feel they have experienced transformative learning? And second, if so, what factors do they perceive to be responsible for bringing about the transformation (or lack of it)? For such an evaluation, it is important to use an instrument based on a theoretical framework that is more holistic and allows us to gather data on the extent of perceived transformative learning as well as possible perceived factors that may predict or explain the extent of transformative learning (or the lack of it).

This research briefly discusses Mezirow's transformative learning theory and a few of the other key theories of adult learning. It then proposes a theoretical framework based on a holistic approach to transformative learning. Using that framework, a revised transformative learning survey instrument was proposed, which was used to gather data on the extent of perceived

---

11. Taylor, "Transformative Learning: Neurobiological Perspective," 231.
12. Dirkx, Mezirow, and Cranton, "Musings and Reflections," 133.
13. Shaw, *Transforming Theological Education*.

transformative learning and the perceived factors for transformative learning within select evangelical theological educational institutions in Ethiopia.

Statement of the Problem

The purpose of theological education is to strengthen the work of the church as it trains men and women who are capable of guiding and empowering the church to be effective in fulfilling its mission.[14] The extent to which the graduates from theological educational institutions experience a holistic transformation may affect their contribution to the transformative ministry of the church and its impact in the world.

Although the idea of transformative learning became an important development in adult education since Jack Mezirow, a review of the literature shows that there is little research done to study transformative learning within higher theological educational institutions. There is no evidence of research done on transformative learning within the Ethiopian formal higher theological education context. This research will broaden the studies done on transformative learning in different contexts. King, who has done an extensive study in the area of transformative learning and has developed the original Learning Activities Survey (LAS), quotes here own work saying,

> The need to replicate this study in other settings and among different populations cannot be overlooked. Important information about perspective transformation could be gathered as responses are analyzed from different types of universities, other adult education programs, different geographical regions, different cultures, and different countries. The similarities and differences among the perspective transformation experience would provide insight into adult learning theory, teaching methods, and educational practice. The "Learning Activities Survey" could be used in its present form or modified to meet specific needs for the sake of such inquiry.[15]

---

14. Shaw, *Transformative Theological Education*; Ferris, Lillis, and Enlow, *Ministry Education*.

15. King, "Examining Learning Activities," 23–37, quoted in King, *Handbook of Evolving Research*, Kindle Locations 5158–5159.

Susan Madsen and Bradley Cook – who modified and used King's Learning Activities Survey (LAS) to measure transformative learning in the UAE with a focus on women in higher education – also recommend replication of the study in order to expand the generalizability of the findings.[16]

This research seeks to expand the extensive work that is already done in other contexts on the topic of transformative learning. It assesses the extent students within Ethiopian evangelical theological higher educational institutions perceive to have experienced transformative learning and the possible factors they perceive that may have contributed to its development or the lack of it.

Research Purpose

This is a mixed method of study seeking to determine the predictive factors that may contribute to students' self-reported transformation or the lack of it as a result of their study at select ACTEA-related theological institutions in Ethiopia. A triangulation mixed methods design will be used, and it will involve collecting both quantitative and qualitative data concurrently.[17]

In order to accomplish this purpose, this study proposes a holistic theoretical framework that suggests the interaction of the three domains of learning (cognitive, affect, and behavior) throughout the process of transformative learning, which has five interactive stages. Concepts from Mezirow's transformational learning theory, Kolb's experiential learning theory, and Duane Elmer's learning cycle were used in developing these stages.

Background of the Colleges Included in the Study

There are five colleges included in this study. They are selected for this study based on their relationship with ACTEA (Association of Christian Theological Education in Africa), which is an accrediting institution for Africa. A brief description of each of the colleges is given in this section.

---

16. Madsen and Cook, "Transformative Learning."
17. Gay, Mills, and Airasian, *Educational Research*, 491.

Shiloh Bible College Ethiopia

Shiloh Bible College Ethiopia (SBCE) was established as an expansion of Shiloh Bible College in the United States of America, which was founded by Dr. Violet Kiteley in the 1960s. Shiloh Bible College Ethiopia opened and offered its first class in 1994. It was established with the vision

> to glorify God by providing excellent and biblically sound theological education for Christian women and men to prepare them to be mature, anointed, God-centered Christian servant leaders and missionaries who will both live out and teach the full counsel of God thereby producing God-honoring, obedient disciples of Christ in the nation of Ethiopia and beyond.[18]

Its Bachelor of Arts in Theology program is designed around three ministry majors: Biblical and Theological Studies, Christian Leadership Studies and Missional Studies. The purpose of the program is "to prepare well-equipped servant leaders and ministers for the church of God based on their calling and the need of the church in Ethiopia and beyond."[19] It has a candidacy status with ACTEA and awaiting its full accreditation soon.[20]

Ethiopian Full Gospel Theological Seminary

The Ethiopian Full Gospel Theological Seminary (EFGTS) was built on the vision of its founding organization, Ethiopian Full Gospel Believers Church in 1988, to "help, train, develop, and mobilize Christian leaders in Ethiopia and around the world on the way to fulfill the Great Commission of Christ."[21]

It offers a Bachelor of Arts in Bible and Theology; Master of Theology in Biblical and Theological Studies, Intercultural Studies, and Practical Theology; Master of Philosophy in Inter-cultural Studies; Master of Divinity in Biblical-Theological Studies and Practical Theology; and Doctor of Theology with Biblical and Theological focus and Practical Theology. The seminary has a candidacy status with ACTEA, and it has signed partnership agreements

---

18. Shiloh Bible College Ethiopia, "Prospectus."
19. Shiloh Bible College Ethiopia, 27.
20. ACTEA, "Accredited Programs and Institutions."
21. EFGTS, "Curriculum and Programs," accessed 16 July 2019, http://www.efgts.org/.

with the South African Theological Seminary (SATS) and the University of the Free State (UFS).[22]

The seminary runs its program on the main campus in Addis Ababa but also runs on different campuses across the country. It is believed that close to 97 percent of its graduates are engaged in full-time ministry.

Meserete Kristos College

The Meserete Kristos church experienced an astronomical growth during the communist regime. The founding of the Meserete Kristos College (MKC) in 1994 was necessary to produce leaders for this growing church. During the communist regime when the church was growing and needing trained leaders, the Meserete Kristos church responded by establishing a committee that provided informal leadership training to the underground church and hence a Bible school "without walls" was organized. As the ministry of this school grew, and the church continued to grow, the church established MKC in 1994.[23]

The purpose of the institution was "to provide relevant and contextualized biblical training for the pastors, evangelists and other leaders within Ethiopia."[24] In 1997 the Bible Institute was reorganized as the Meserete Kristos College. The college offers a four-year Baccalaureate degree in Bible and Christian ministries and a distance education program offering diploma level instruction in Bible and Christian Ministries. It has candidate status with ACTEA and partnership for accreditation with Eastern Mennonite University.[25]

Mekane Yesus Seminary

The Mekane Yesus Seminary (MYS) website explains that the seminary was established to serve its founding church (Ethiopian Evangelical Church Mekane Yesus). It sought to fulfill the objective "of training leaders, ministers, and teachers for the various ministries of the EECMY, Churches in Ethiopia and beyond."[26] This task is to be carried out by arranging courses on different

---

22. EFGTS, "Curriculum and Programs."
23. Meserete Kristos College, "Who We Are."
24. Meserete Kristos College.
25. Meserete Kristos College.
26. Mekane Yesus Seminary, "Mekane Yesus Seminary History," About, http://mekaneyesusseminary.org/purpose/.

levels to meet the needs in both rural and urban settings. The intention of MYS is that its students would equip church workers to do effective Christian ministries within the unique context of the Ethiopian culture. Although the church provided training during the Italian occupation in the 1940s and afterward, it officially started its ministry in September 1960.[27]

It has three departments, namely, the Department of Theology, the Mekane Yesus Management and Leadership College, and the Music and Theological Education by Extension. The theology department offers both undergraduate and graduate-level training. It offers its program at its main campus in Addis Ababa but also in Bishoftu. It has full accreditation with the ACTEA for its Diploma of Theology, Bachelor of Theology as well as Master of Arts in Theology programs.[28]

Evangelical Theological College

The Evangelical Theological College is owned by the Ethiopian Kale Heywot Church (EKHC). It was started in 1983 in response to the need for trained leaders in the growing underground church during the communist regime.[29]

Its purpose is "to prepare servant leaders for the church in Ethiopia and beyond." In order to do this, it offers a Bachelor of Theology program, Master of Arts in Holistic Child Development, Educational Leadership, and Youth Ministry. Although the college is owned by a denomination, it trains students coming from diverse denominational backgrounds. Its Bachelor of Theology program is fully accredited by ACTEA and it is pursuing accreditation for its graduate programs with ACTEA.[30]

Research Questions and Hypotheses

The study seeks to answer the following research questions:

1. To what extent do students studying at ACTEA-related theological colleges in Ethiopia perceive themselves to have had a transformative learning experience?

---

27. MYS, "About Us."
28. MYS, "About Us."
29. ETC, "About Us."
30. ETC, "Programs."

2. To what extent do instructional strategies predict or explain self-reported transformative learning in students studying at ACTEA-related theological colleges in Ethiopia?

    H_o1: There is no statistically significant relationship between the perceived transformative learning and the instructional strategies used within ACTEA-related theological institutions in Ethiopia.

3. Is there is a difference between the teachers' and the students' perceptions of the instructional strategies that predict students' transformative learning experience?

    H_o2: There is no statistically significant difference in the perceptions of the students and the teachers on the predictive relationship of the perceived transformative learning and the instructional strategies used within ACTEA-related theological institutions.

4. To what extent do student interactions with other individuals in the college predict or explain self-reported transformative learning experience in students studying at ACTEA-related theological colleges in Ethiopia?

    H_o3: There is no statistically significant relationship between the students' perceived transformative learning and their interactions with other individuals within the college.

5. To what extent is the self-reported transformative learning experience of students in full-time study different from those in part-time studies?

    H_o4: There is no statistically significant difference in the perceived transformative learning experience between students in full-time study and those in part-time study.

Limitations and Delimitations of the Study

1. The study is based on the self-report of the students from theological institutions. Therefore, the data collected is dependent on their ability to accurately remember their experiences.

The Problem and Its Setting

2. The focus of the study is on students who are in undergraduate programs that are accredited or working towards full accreditation with ACTEA. Therefore, a number of the other theological colleges that are not accredited by ACTEA, but are training leaders for the church in Ethiopia, are not included in this study.
3. Students' transformative learning experience is assessed in light of their perceived concerted transformation in cognitive, affective, and behavioral. It would not include other possible factors such as personal motivation, sociopolitical factors, spiritual elements to transformation, etc.
4. The study is also limited to factors contributing to students' transformative learning experiences within the college or related to the college. It does not consider other possible factors outside of the activities related to the theological institutions such as the students' engagement in ministry, personal spiritual discipline, the backgrounds the students come with, etc.

Definition of Terms

It is possible that different terminologies may be understood differently. This section gives operational definitions that are used for some of the key terms in this research.

> *Andragogy* – the art and science of assisting adults to learn. "An organized and sustained effort to assist adults to learn in a way that enhances their capability to function as self-directed learners."[31]

Learning is believed to occur in three distinct but inter-related domains – namely, cognitive, affective, and behavioral or psychomotor. Shaw defines the three domains of learning as follows.[32]

> *Affective learning* – learning that shapes values, attitudes, emotions, and motivations.
>
> *Behavioral learning* – learning that shapes one's actions and skills.

---

31. Mezirow, *Transformative Dimensions*, 199.
32. Shaw, *Transforming Theological Education*, 69.

Cognitive learning – learning that results in the development of complex thinking skills.

Dispositions (also referred to as habits) – "precognitive tendencies to act in certain ways and toward certain ends."[33] Shaw describes dispositions to be the result of the concerted action of cognition, affect, and behavior.[34]

Learning – a number of educators would agree that the one-word definition of learning is "change." The definition of learning should include both a process as well as a state of being that results from the process. A combination of Gagne's definition[35] and that of Mezirow's provides the definition that is used in this study. Learning is a more or less permanent disposition gained through the process of using a prior interpretation to construe a new or a revised interpretation of the meaning of one's experience in order to guide future action.[36] In this study, future action includes the revision of a point of view, modification of an attitude, or a change in behavior.

Transformative learning – in this study, transformative learning is learning that aims at a concerted transformation of the three dimensions of one's disposition in any learning process – the revision of point of view, modification of an attitude, or a change in behavior.[37]

Transformative learning experience – this is the extent students have experienced transformative learning.

The frame of reference – the structures of assumptions and premises through which experiences are understood. They shape

---

33. Smith, *Desiring the Kingdom*, 55.
34. Shaw, *Transforming Theological Education*, 76.
35. Robert M. Gagne, *The Conditions of Learning*, quoted in Curzon, *Teaching in Further Education*, 11.
36. Mezirow, *Transformative Dimensions*, 12.
37. Mezirow, "Transformative Learning"; Shaw, *Transforming Theological Education*.

expectations, perceptions, cognition, feelings, and set one's "line of action"[38]

Redemptive teaching – teaching in a fashion that reflects the character of the creative-redemptive God. "Creative" and "redemptive" suggest that we are to teach in accord with God's creational ordinances and in a way that demonstrates his grace in redemption."[39]

Research Assumptions

This research is based on student perceptions. Therefore, one of the assumptions is that the students are able to understand and rate the items on the research instrument accurately and that they will do so with integrity. Furthermore, it assumes that three to four years of study at the college has given the students sufficient learning experience in order to provide a useful and accurate response to the survey.

It also assumes that since the colleges involved in the study are all accredited or at a certain stage of being accredited by ACTEA, they have similar standards for student admissions, qualifications of the faculty, and the facilities available for learning.

Finally, it is assumed that it is impossible to fully categorize how people learn. As Perry Shaw says, "learning is complex, and the physical, emotional, relational, cognitive, moral and spiritual aspects of the human person are closely intertwined."[40] Therefore, the framework proposed in this research is far from being exhaustive.

Summary of the Research Process

This research is a mixed method employing both descriptive and inferential statistics. An instrument was developed to survey the degree of perceived transformative learning and the possible factors that may predict or explain

---

38. Mezirow, "Transformative Learning," 5.
39. Graham, *Teaching Redemptively*, xv.
40. Shaw, *Transforming Theological Education*, 69.

transformative learning. The instrument was developed by revising the instrument developed by Dr. Kathleen King.

The revision of the LAS was necessary because of the different theoretical framework for transformative learning that guides this research and with the intent of making it more suitable for the evangelical theological educational context in Ethiopia. The theoretical framework used in this study will be discussed later in the literature review section. Since the revised survey instrument had significant alterations, it was tested for validity and reliability prior to using it for the research. Dr. King has given her permission to the researcher to be able to use the LAS instrument for the purpose of this research.

The researcher contacted the head of the five theological colleges, selected by the sampling process stated in the population and sampling section, in order to receive permission to carry out the research. Once that permission was granted, the researcher worked with the academic deans and the registrars at the colleges to identify the students in their graduating years to participate in the study. The selection process will be explained in more detail in chapter 3. The students were given the survey to complete, and the researcher encouraged them to return the completed survey forms by providing a small incentive in appreciation of their time.

A focus group discussion was conducted at each of the colleges with eight randomly selected students from among those who returned the survey forms. The questions used in the survey guided the focus group discussion to gather more in-depth perspectives on the issues.

In order to gain the perspectives of the teachers, the researcher designed a survey, which had questions similar to the students' survey. This helped in triangulating the responses of the students with that of the teachers. A t-test was conducted to identify possible differences between the responses of the instructors and the students in relation to the activities perceived to predict transformative learning.

Significance of the Study

The purpose of the evangelical theological colleges in Ethiopia is to produce men and women who are capable of guiding and empowering the church to be effective in fulfilling its mission. The results of this study will inform the theological institutions of the extent students perceive to have experienced transformative learning while studying at the institutions. It will also provide information on some of the factors that may have contributed to the transformative learning experience students had or the lack of it. The researcher believes that the understanding of the factors will help the theological institutions create an environment that provides more opportunities for students to experience transformative learning while studying at the colleges. With an improved quality of learning, there will be an improved quality of graduates.

Although the Ethiopian context may be different from others, the factors that are identified in this study may be generalized to some extent to other contexts as well by building on what others have already done in the area of transformative learning. It is also the hope of the researcher that the revised instrument may be helpful to those who seek to do a similar study in the field.

The literature review will discuss the biblical perspective of transformative learning, the literature on transformative and adult learning theories, and will conclude with a brief presentation of literature on instructional strategies and the contributions of interpersonal relationships to transformative learning. The subsequent chapters will provide an explanation of the research methodology, the findings, and the conclusions of the study.

CHAPTER 2

Literature Review

Introduction

There is not enough space and time to cover all the literature that is written on transformative learning. This section of the study includes a discussion of the biblical foundation for understanding transformative learning, select transformative and adult learning theories, and literature on instructional strategies and interpersonal relationships.

The literature review will then briefly summarize Jack Mezirow's idea of transformative learning from his original writings. It will also include the works of those who have wrestled with the topic and have added different aspects to the understanding of transformative learning. While Mezirow's work is primarily a cognitive process, other works that suggest affect and behavior (practice) as their focus for transformative learning will be considered. Finally, the works done on adult learning theories will also be covered in this literature review, which will contribute to the understanding of a transformative learning process.

Theological Foundations for Transformative Learning

He is almost there, he can see it from a distance, and he has led the people to it, but he is not going to be in it. He will only see it from a distance. But the people he led will be going into it. He knows how easily the people are likely to turn away from God, who has graciously led them to this point and so, he says, "Hear, O Israel: the LORD our God the LORD is one" (Deut 6:4). What is it that Moses wanted them to hear? What was most important for him to say at this time of his life? It was the need to recognize and acknowledge that the LORD is the one and only God and there is none other. The Israelites are entering into a land where many gods are acknowledged as gods. The Israelites needed to set Yahweh as the one true God. The acknowledgment of the Lord as the one God must be followed up with three appropriate responses.

The first response is found in the statement, "You shall love the LORD your God with all your heart and with all your soul and with all your might" (Deut. 6:5). Coley and Turner, in summarizing their explanation of what Moses is saying in the commandment in Deuteronomy 6, say, "Obey the Lord your God exclusively with all your innermost personal reflections; with all your outermost public expressions; and with all your efforts and exertions."[1] In describing the innermost reflections, they explain that the Hebrew word *levav* (heart and mind) "is a one-word designation for all the inner dimensions of a person that God alone sees – one's attitude, thinking processes, affections, and feelings. The command to love the Lord with all that is deep within oneself." The word *nephesh* (soul and life), "describes all the outer dimensions of a person – the aspects that other people see, hear, and experience. It is behavior, actions, work, and words."[2] From their explanation, it can be concluded that change is what happens both from the inside (heart and mind) and also on the outside (behavior). The Israelites were to respond with both an inward as well as an outward change in their lives.

Moses goes on to give them the second response, "And these words that I command you today shall be on your heart" (Deut 6:6). The Psalmist says, "Your word is a lamp to my feet and a light to my path" (Ps 119:105). The inward and outward change is possible as the word of God guides believers in the path they must walk and protects them from living a life of sin – as expressed by the Psalmist, "I have stored up your word in my heart, that I might not sin against you" (Ps 119:11).

The climax of the internal transformation is demonstrated in the third response, as Moses tells the Israelites, "You shall teach them diligently to your children, and shall talk of them when you sit in your house . . ." (Deut 6:7).

---

1. Coley and Turner, "Examining Deuteronomy 6," 8.
2. Coley and Turner, 8.

Teaching is the outward demonstration of one's inward commitment to God and a life transformed by the word of God. The inward transformation cannot exist separate from the outward expression of it as much as the outward expression cannot exist apart from the inward transformation. They are both inseparably interrelated.

Unfortunately, it has been the experience of the researcher that traditional Ethiopian educational system places a great emphasis on the inward change, more specifically, on the memorization of content. This approach to education does not require the development of creativity and critical thinking skills. This is also a feature that is observed within the churches and theological educational institutions in Ethiopia. As LeBar[3] says, many hear the word of God and go out to do nothing about it. The teacher does not really expect anything to happen, and the learners do not expect anything to happen. In speaking of the traditional approach to education within theological educational institutions, Paul Sanders says, "The problem with much of theological education is that it is neither theological nor educational."[4] The evangelical theological beliefs need to be investigated for their implications to the educational practice in theological education.

When reflecting on the theological foundation for theological education, three questions should be considered.

1. What does theological education seek to accomplish in its students?
2. Why does it aim for that?
3. How does it seek to accomplish that?

Rupen Das explains the process of theological education using what he refers to as the logic chain, as shown in figure 1.[5]

---

3. LeBar, *Education*, 99.

4. Sanders, "Evangelical Theological Education," quoted in Shaw, *Transforming Theological Education*, 15.

5. Das, *Connecting Curriculum*, 41.

A Logic Chain

ACTIVITY Action/training/etc.	→	OUTPUT Change as a result of the activity (individual level)	→	OUTCOME Change as a result of the output (community level)	→	IMPACT longer term societal change (context of the larger society)

Figure 1: A logic chain model

Shaw adds the element "input" to Das's chain and describes the components of this chain as follows:

> "Inputs" (physical plant, book resources, finances, and people), support the "activities" (the curriculum), that would lead to desired "output" (graduates who have changed as a result of their studies), that in turn leads to positive "outcomes" (churches that are more faithful and effective in their missional calling), that result in "impact" on society.[6]

It is important to notice that the output represents the transformed graduates. The second point to notice is that the graduates experience transformation as a result of the activities and their degree of engagement in those activities while at the college. Finally, the purpose of the graduates' transformation is termed in the logic chain as the outcome, which is to see churches that are more faithful and effective in their missional calling.

In this section, the researcher will discuss the implications of the evangelical theological system of beliefs for the desired output, the intended outcome, and the methodology that must be considered in order to see the desired output.

Transformation – the Purpose of Theological Education

The purpose of learning is not just that one would have information but rather experience holistic transformation. The purpose of learning is "transformation, realized as truth incorporated into life . . . it must be enacted in the life

---

6. Shaw, "Holistic and Transformative," 209.

of the learner before it is acknowledged as learned."[7] The holistic nature of learning requires understanding learning as being more than just cognition but more of a "heart relationship and obedient action. To know God is to be changed by God."[8]

The biblical understanding of knowledge is closely tied to the act of obedience. The Israelites were given the commandments so that they would obey it and by their obedience, they may be set apart for God among the nations (Deut 28; Josh 1:8). The learning of the commandments required them to respond in obedience. Jesus and the apostles taught so that people would repent of their way of life. The apostle John tells his readers the reason for writing his gospel was that "you may believe that Jesus is the Messiah, the Son of God, and that by believing you may have life in his name" (20:31 NIV).

Theological education that results in learner transformation necessitates a theological reflection on what theological educational institutions are doing and how they go about it. If it is to be truly theological education, it is necessary that andragogical principles are established on the proper understanding of biblical theology.

The Need for Graduate Transformation

Jesus spent three years with his disciples revealing the Father to them and training them. However, his purpose did not stop with them knowing God and being trained as his disciples. Rather, he sent them out into the world as sheep among the wolves with the great commission to make disciples of the nations, teaching them to obey everything that he had commanded them (Matt 28:19).

In stating the mission of theological education, the Lausanne Movement's Cape Town Commitment states, "The mission of the church on earth is to serve the mission of God, and the mission of theological education is to strengthen and accompany the mission of the church."[9] God is a missionary-God sending the church on a mission to the world. As the church does its missional work, partnering with the church and giving strength to the ministry of the church is the focus of theological education.

---

7. Ferris, Lillis, and Enlow, *Ministry Education*, 14.

8. Shaw, *Transforming Theological Education*, 69.

9. Lausanne Movement, "Cape Town Commitment," II.F.4.

Das, in speaking of the purpose of the theological educational institution says,

> Is the focus to train the students to become pastors who are able to do the work of the ministry through activities such as evangelism, leading Bible Studies, counseling, and preaching? Or is the focus on training the students to enable and equip church members to mature in Christ so that they are able to do the work of ministry (Eph. 4:12–15)? If the focus is only on the students to become a pastor, then any evaluation of the effectiveness of the institution is based on whether the student completed the curriculum and was successfully trained. If the focus of training is on the graduate being able to equip a local church "for the work of ministry," then an evaluation of the effectiveness of the curriculum does not end with the student successfully graduating, but on the graduate's progress to equip the church where they minister.[10]

Paul can also be heard telling the church that God has given spiritual gifts to the believers "to equip his people for works of service, so that the body of Christ may be built up" (Eph 4:11–13). The transformation of the graduates is for the purpose of building up the body of Christ – the church.

Biblical Understanding of Man – Foundations for Transformative Learning

A teacher's belief in the nature of man shapes the teacher-student interactions and educational practices. Fritz Deininger says, "Theological and educational commitments grow out of the statement of faith. They affirm the values that are lived out in the learning community by the teachers as well as by the students."[11] The statement of faith of the evangelical theological educational institutions should have several elements to it. This study focuses on the nature of humanity in order to see how the andragogical practices should be influenced by the right understanding of humankind, as God's image-bearers and redeemed through the redemptive work of the Lord Jesus Christ.

---

10. Das, *Connecting Curriculum*, 2.
11. Deininger, "Foundations for Curriculum," 16.

The image of God in humankind and its implications to theological education

Humans are created in the image of God (Gen 1:26), which makes them unique from all creation. The uniqueness of humanity is demonstrated in the functional responsibility humans are given to exercise dominion over all of God's creation, choose to remain in obedience to God, and exercise their capacity for free will. If humankind's uniqueness in creation is affirmed, then it is important to ask how the understanding of humanity's creation in the image of God should affect the process of education. How should the purpose for which theological training is offered in seminaries or Bible teaching in the churches be different because of the belief that humankind is created in the image of God? What significant difference should the idea of redemption make in the purpose of teaching, curriculum design, and teaching strategies? How are students impacted by the end of a course or a certain program of study? If all that happens is that they have completed the program with high distinction but have not experienced transformation in their life and ministry, which allows them to be meaningfully engaged in the society, then we have failed as a church and as a seminary.[12]

The fact that humans are created in the image of God should cause teachers to reconsider their perceptions of the components of education for transformative classroom instruction. If Christian educators honestly believe their theology of humanity as the image-bearers of God, then their theology should drive their educational practices.[13] In the following few pages, the nature of humankind as God's image-bearers and its implications to transformative learning will be discussed.

Understanding the image of God in humanity. In trying to understand the meaning of the image of God in humankind, three views have been proposed over time. First, the substantive view suggests that the image is related to ontological capacities such as intelligence, will, and freedom. A second view is what is referred to as the relational view where the image is considered to be related to humans' unique ability to relate to others and God. Finally, there is the functional view, which argues that the image of God is related to humanity's dominion over God's creation. Although all positions have

---

12. Shaw, "Holistic and Transformative," 209.
13. Shaw, 209.

good grounds for their arguments, as Estep, Anthony, and Allison tell us the problem is that all of these views

> tend to reduce the image of God to one particular part or aspect of our humanness; thus, they miss the key point: we human beings are not made in a piecemeal way and put together, like the many pieces of a jig-saw puzzle, to become what we are. Rather, in our humanness, we are constructed holistically with wholeness and completeness that does not allow us to be divided into this part and that part.[14]

Keathley and Rooker quote Wayne Grudem who says, "the image of God may simply refer to every way in which man is like God."[15] C. F. H. Henry said, "Humanity is made for personal and endless fellowship with God, involving rational understanding (Gen. 1:28–29), moral obedience (2:16–17), and religious communion (3:3). Humanity is given dominion over the animals and charged to subdue the earth, that is, to consecrate it to the spiritual service of God and humankind."[16]

David Akin, in his chapter titled "We Are Created in the Image of God," provides some guidelines to remember in understanding the image of God in humans. He tells us that although the image of God is affirmed for all persons, "the likeness is not made very specific, it is the basis for human uniqueness and dignity, it is not completely lost in the fall and finally the image of God is not only our created design but also our eschatological destiny."[17]

It can, therefore, be concluded that man is created in the image of God in all areas: in his capacity to make rational decisions, to rule over God's creation, and to relate with God and others. Donovan L. Graham, in his book *Teaching Redemptively: Bringing Grace and Truth into Your Classroom*, gives us some of the following specific implications to the nature of man at creation.[18]

Active and purposeful. Just as God is active in creation and its continued sustenance, humans are also active in creating ideas and things, making sense of things in relation to themselves, in an effort to exercise some manner of

---

14. Estep, Anthony, and Allison, *Theology for Christian Education*, 180.
15. Grudem, *Systematic Theology*, 443, quoted in Keathley and Rooker, *40 Questions*, 235.
16. Henry, "Image of God," 593, quoted in Keathley and Rooker, *40 Questions*, 235.
17. Akin, *Theology for the Church*, ch. 7, WORDsearch.
18. Graham, *Teaching Redemptively*, 73–88.

control over the world humankind is commanded to subdue. Our actions are guided by a specific purpose that we have although the purpose may not seem to be in the direction of God.

Creative, rational being. Packer is quoted in Graham saying that creation was the result of a mind "thinking, forming, and evaluating."[19] God has created man and woman in such a way that they can exhibit rationality in exercising rule over creation as directed by God. They reflect the rational character of God though they do so in a distorted and ineffective way. Students who share in the attribute of rationality have the capacity to think, which is woven into the fabric of their existence and so they need to be treated as such. Men and women exercise creativity in all the activities of life where the mind, emotions, and will are used to form and utilize concepts and material things. They utilize what God has created and placed in the universe informing every aspect of culture. They are also constantly making value judgments about the new ideas and things others have created.[20]

Free and responsible. God acts freely according to his purposes, making choices to do as he wills. Humans also exercise their freedom by making choices within the limit of their finiteness. With freedom also comes responsibility for the choices one makes. Every choice one makes comes with its own positive or negative consequences for which the person is responsible. The educational process must be one that also provides students with choices and one that allows the students to live with the consequences of the choices they make. This is as opposed to the perception that teaching is simply telling students what they need to believe and do.[21]

Relational by nature. God has created humans as relational beings functioning in a relationship with nature and each other. They function as stewards of God's creation, socially involved, and express love, and mercy to others to a varying degree. As the stewards of God's creation, men and women exercise a measure of control over the environment and created things. Their stewardship also includes developing a culture by creating governments, aesthetic products, and all other dimensions of culture. God's expectation from those who are placed as stewards is to provide care and nurture for his creation.

---

19. Packer, *Knowing Man*, quoted in Graham, *Teaching Redemptively*, 75.
20. Graham, *Teaching Redemptively*, 77.
21. Graham, 80.

Education must, therefore, be designed in such a way that men and women learn to meet God's expectations in caring for his creation and also influencing culture in a manner that brings glory to God.[22]

Being social in nature, students would also benefit from an educational process that is designed to foster the development of fellowship and working together as opposed to setting a competitive environment that has a negative effect on the community. Within this context of fellowship with one another, there must also be a demonstration of love and mercy towards one another. These are characters that need to be demonstrated by the teacher but equally exhibited by the students in their relationship with one another.[23]

Understanding the effect of the fall on the image. The fall has affected the image of God in humanity, but it is not destroyed completely. Their gifts, endowments, and capacities were not destroyed by the fall – but they now began to use these gifts in ways that were contrary to God's will.[24] The effect of the fall can be seen in the broken relationship with God as men and women gave themselves to the worship and praise of idols, the works of their own hands. They use their moral capacities in a perverted manner calling what is wrong, right and what is right, wrong. The fall has also affected their relationship with others as a they use their gifts to manipulate, use others for personal gain, and exploit them. Finally, their responsibility to rule over God's creation has been affected as they exercise their dominion in sinful ways.[25]

Understanding the restoration of the image. Because of the redemptive work of God through Jesus, the image of God is being restored through the work of the Holy Spirit and it will find its completion only at the time of the resurrection.[26]

Through the work of the Holy Spirit humans experience renewal of the fallen nature. Anthony A. Hoekema gives us some of the areas where they begin to experience renewal. The first area is in their relationship with God. While they were directed to rebellion against God, they are now enabled to turn towards God and respond in worship through their obedience. In their

---

22. Graham, 83–84.
23. Graham, 84–88.
24. Hoekema, *Created in God's Image*, ch. 5, WORDsearch.
25. Hoekema, ch. 5.
26. Hoekema, ch. 5.

relationship with one another, they are also able to seek the good of others in love using their rational and volitional powers to care for others. Restoration will also mean that humankind will be able to exercise dominion over creation in a manner that is glorifying to God. Finally, they also experience restoration in the development of culture as believers engage in philosophical, scientific, historical, and literary work in a Christian way that develops culture influenced by Christian worldviews.[27]

Implications of restoration to the role of the teacher and student.

Learning must start with the understanding of human nature, without which it will not be possible to proceed and understand the nature of the task in education. A clear understanding of the nature of humanity as God's image-bearers helps in understanding God's purpose in education.[28] Greg Allison, in his book *A Theology for Christian Education*, gives some of the implications of the understanding of humans as God's image-bearers within the framework of creation, fall, and redemption.[29]

Education for God's purpose. The purpose of education is to see that students, within the teaching ministries of the church or seminaries, experience transformation into the likeness of Jesus. The apostle Paul tells us, "Do not be conformed to this world, but be transformed by the renewal of your mind" (Rom 12:1). The ultimate goal for Paul is that the believers will be holy (set apart from the society around them).

It is important to recognize from the outset that God's purpose for transformation happens through the authoritative word of God and the work of the Holy Spirit both in the teacher and the students. In order for this to happen, transformation should begin in the life of the teacher. It is as the teachers allow themselves to be filled with the word of God, and ministered to by the Holy Spirit, that they will become instruments for the transformation of others. Where this is not happening, the teachers may, in fact, end up being hindrances to the transforming work that God desires to do in the lives of the students.[30]

---

27. Hoekema, ch. 5.
28. Wilson, *Recovering the Lost*, 69.
29. Allison, "Humanity, Sin," 174–99.
30. Allison, 191–92.

Education that facilitates a holistic response. Students are not mere "heads" to unlatch, open up, and pour content into; imparting knowledge is not enough. Education must be one that involves the appropriation, development, and expression of sanctified thoughts, emotions, decisions, actions, motivations, and purposes. This can happen as people experience transformation through teaching under the power of the Holy Spirit. Such kind of teaching will require modeling and a personal relationship with students.[31]

The communication of information is important for students to begin their process of transformation. However, students must respond to the information not only by repeating the information but by demonstrating their understanding of the concepts they learn. The response must also be observed emotionally. Douglas Wilson tells us that, "true classical learning takes place when students come to love what they retain. This can only happen if the teachers love their subjects."[32] The information students gain must be responded to emotionally, which is caught from the attitude of the teacher. Such an emotional conviction to an understanding of a concept should then lead to practicing the newly learned concept. Students have not learned, and teachers have not taught until the students begin to demonstrate it holistically.

Education in human relationship. Relationships are significant elements in the learning process. The relationships between the teacher and the students and the ones among the students themselves have significant contributions to the learning process. The teachers should not be seeking to gain their significance from the relationships they have with their students, but rather they must have their own source for meeting their relational needs with others as well as with God. Out of the overflow of that, the teachers become a catalyst to facilitate healthy relationships among the students.[33]

As Paul indicates in Ephesians 4:32, the relationships with students must be characterized by love, patience, forbearance, and forgiveness. It must not discriminate between the students to cause harm to one. At the same time, it is important to differentiate in order to design teaching to meet the needs of each individual. Therefore, the human relations aspect looks at the possibilities of caring for each individual student within the classroom.

---

31. Allison, 189.
32. Wilson, *Recovering the Lost*, 79.
33. Allison, "Humanity, Sin."

Wilson adds to this by saying that the fallenness of humans must not be mistaken for absolute depravity. Students, though fallen, still have the image of God and hence need to be treated with dignity. The teacher must demonstrate respect for the students both in the preparation for teaching as well as in the relationships with the students.[34]

Education within human development. The level of transformation a person may achieve is determined by the developmental level the person has already attained. Developmental scientists such as Jean Piaget, Lev Vygotsky, Erik Erickson, Lawrence Kohlberg, and James Fowler have put forward developmental theories on the developmental processes. Although these developmental theories are not able to deal with sin or bring about the restoration of relationship with God, they can, however, aid teachers to design learning experiences that are fit for the developmental levels of their students.[35]

Rightly positioned. Students, as God's image-bearers, come with a reservoir of experience and are capable of reasoning. The teachers do not need to present themselves as the redeemers while the students are perceived to be completely lost. This means that teachers and students can have a dialogue within a classroom. Paulo Freire describes the lack of this dialogue in the classroom by comparing the teacher-student relationship to the relationship between a slave and the master where dialogue is not possible.[36] However, it should not be so in the classrooms if transformation is to happen. Freire says,

> The important thing is to help me (and nations) help themselves, to place them in consciously critical confrontation with their problems, to make them the agents of their own recuperation. In contrast, assistencialism robs men of a fundamental human necessity – responsibility.[37]

Students learn as they are actively engaged in their own learning process. The relationship between the teacher and student must be "I-thou relationship, and thus necessarily a relationship between two subjects. Each time the 'thou' is changed into an object, an 'it,' dialogue is subverted, and education

---

34. Wilson, *Recovering the Lost*, 70.
35. Allison, "Humanity, Sin."
36. Freire, *Education for Critical Consciousness*; Freire, *Pedagogy of the Oppressed*.
37. Freire, *Pedagogy of the Oppressed*, 16.

is changed to deformation."[38] This does not mean there is no place for the teacher to give instruction or that the teacher is not more knowledgeable than the student is but rather, it is to say that the student is equally made in the image of God with the capacity for rational thinking and hence with proper guidance, the students can be made active participants in their own learning.

Conclusion

Theological education provides opportunities for learners to experience transformation as they are exposed to the teachings of God's truth through the creative guidance of the teacher and the work of the Holy Spirit. A group of disciples were gathered in a room and they were filled with grief because they had lost their master. They saw their master killed and placed in a tomb, and all their hopes had disappeared with him. Suddenly they saw a ghost of him in the room; at least they thought it was a ghost. But it was the Lord Jesus himself. They had a disorienting experience, and they were not sure how to respond. Jesus invited them to check the wounds in his hands and his feet and they responded, and they touched, and they were excited that their Lord was alive. Luke explains that he then "opened their minds to understand the Scriptures" (Luke 24:45). After this experience, they were no longer the hopeless and grieving men hiding in a room. They were changed! They were ready to be witnesses of the gospel to all the nations beginning with Jerusalem (24:40–49).

This is one of the many examples of transformative experiences the disciples had. It involved having an experience that created a need to change and gave them the opportunity to test it under the guidance of the master and it ended with the disciples beginning to act differently because of the experience they had. The experience they had this time was not only a cognitive experience, but rather it involved their affect and the behavior as well.

Theological education is done with the intent of achieving God's purpose of seeing men and women being transformed into the kind of people God desires for them to become. LeBar enforces this in saying that the intention of teaching should be "getting the Person into the Book, and the Book into the Person . . . The Person needs to get involved in the study of it until it gets

---

38. Freire, 52.

into him until he lives in it and it lives in him."[39] The design of the education must be such that it addresses the head but also creates conviction that will, in turn, affect the manner the students behave. It is not God's intent for men and women to be informed, but it is to see lives transformed by the knowledge of God.

Since men and women continue to reflect the image of God in certain respects, the manner of teaching must also reflect that image. If it is believed that students are created to be active and have the capacity for reasoning and rational thinking, then it is important to recognize that transformation does not happen by treating students as passive participants in the learning process. But instead, students must be actively engaged in their own learning process.

The function of theological education does not end with the personal transformation of the learners, but it should move the learners to function in a similar role as that of the teacher (Luke 6:40) of equipping others for works of service (Eph 4:12). This forms the cycle as described in 2 Timothy 2:2, "And the things you have heard me say in the presence of many witnesses entrust to reliable men who will also be qualified to teach others." This cycle is demonstrated in figure 2.

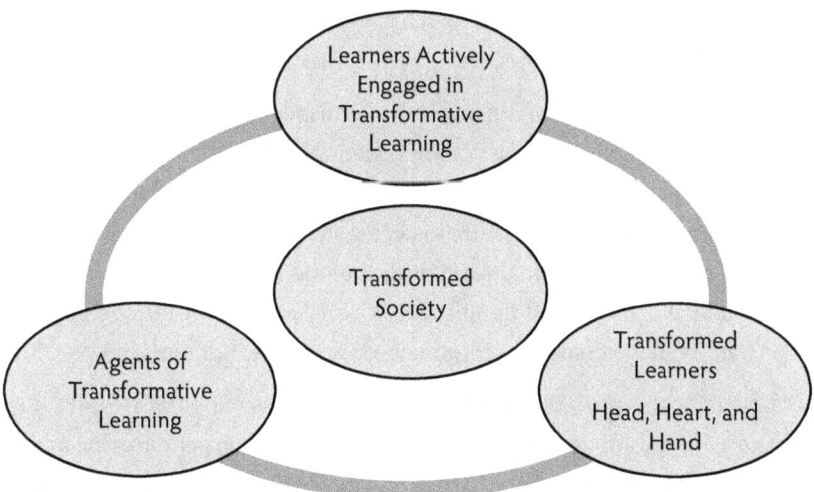

Figure 2: Cycle of transformation based on the logic chain developed by Rupen Das

---

39. LeBar, *Education*, 100.

The following section presents a discussion of Jack Mezirow's theory of transformative learning as well as other alternative transformative learning theories and adult learning theories.

Jack Mezirow's Transformative Learning Theory

Mezirow perceived that although historically psychologists as well as philosophers have had an interest in adult learning, few attempts were made to develop a synthesis of the different theories that adult educators can use. As a result, educators and practitioners were forced to use humanist psychology or behaviorist practices, which were dysfunctional with adult learning. He proposed transformative learning theory as one that completes the dimension that was missing in the psychological theories. Mezirow explained the missing dimension in the existing psychological theories to be "*meaning* – how it is construed, validated, and reformulated – and the social conditions that influence the ways in which adults make meaning of their experience."[40] He argued that a "learning theory centered on meaning, addressed to educators of adults, could provide a firm foundation for a philosophy of adult education from which appropriate practices of goal setting, needs assessment, program development, instruction, and research could be derived."[41] He explains transformative learning as follows:

> Transformative learning involves an enhanced level of awareness of the context of one's beliefs and feelings, a critique of their assumptions and particularly premises, and assessment of alternative perspectives, a decision to negate an old perspective in favor of a new one or to make a synthesis of old and new, and ability to take action based upon the new perspective, and a desire to fit the new perspective into the broader context of one's life.[42]

Crucial to this process is a critical reflection on assumptions. He calls those structures of assumptions and premises through which experiences are understood, the "frames of reference." These frames of reference shape expectations,

---

40. Mezirow, *Transformative Dimensions*, xii.
41. Mezirow, xii.
42. Mezirow, 161.

perceptions, cognition, and feelings and set one's "line of action."[43] A frame of reference encompasses cognitive, conative, and emotional components, and is composed of two dimensions – habits of mind and a point of view. The habits of mind are understood as the broad, abstract, orienting, habitual ways of thinking, feeling, and acting influenced by assumptions that constitute a set of codes, which may be cultural, educational, political, or psychological. He explains the points of view to be the "constellation of belief, value judgments, attitude, and feeling that shapes a particular interpretation."[44]

Cranton explains that transformative learning is a cognitive process where one's perspective (frame of reference) is transformed as a result of a critical reflection on a conflicting experience learners encounter. It is a process of examining, questioning, validating, and revisiting perspectives.[45] Cranton continues to explain that experiences are filtered through habits of mind or meaning perspectives, "which include uncritically assimilated ways of knowing, believing, and feeling."[46] Learning is believed to occur when a student encounters an alternative perspective and prior habits of mind are called into question.[47] Mezirow argues that in a modern society, where rapid, dramatic change and a diversity of beliefs, values, and social practices seem to be a hallmark, the formerly held source of authority and the early learning provided by socialization and schooling will no longer be sufficient for adults to navigate in the changing world. Adults need to acquire new perspectives to deal with the change rather than attempt to apply the old ways of dealing with things. Thus, it becomes necessary that the individual learns to negotiate meanings, purposes, and values critically, reflectively, and rationally instead of passively accepting the social realities defined by others.[48]

Cranton tells us that Mezirow used to believe this transformation to be a single, dramatic event – a disorienting dilemma – but he and others have since acknowledged that it could also be a gradual cumulative process.[49]

---

43. Mezirow, "Transformative Learning," 5.
44. Mezirow, 2.
45. Cranton, *Understanding*, 23.
46. Cranton, 23.
47. Cranton, 23.
48. Mezirow, *Transformative Dimensions*, 17.
49. Cranton, *Understanding*, 23.

Mezirow developed the following stages for perspective transformation after doing a study of women who reentered college to participate in specialized reentry programs.[50]

1. A disorienting dilemma;
2. Self-examination with feelings of guilt or shame;
3. A critical assessment of epistemic, sociocultural, or psychic assumptions;
4. Recognition that one's discontent and the process of transformation are shared and that others have negotiated a similar change;
5. Exploration of opinions for new roles, relationships, and actions;
6. Planning of a course of action;
7. Acquisition of knowledge and skills for implementing one's plans;
8. Provisional trying of new roles;
9. The building of competence and self-confidence in new roles and relationships; and
10. A reintegration into one's life on the basis of conditions dictated by one's new perspective.

King explains that these ten stages represent the full cycle of perspective transformation. She indicates that

> they describe the emotions and efforts that adult learners make to accommodate new information and understanding. It is a time of reflection, change, and action. The process calls for adult learners to critically reflect on their beliefs, values, and understanding, to compare them to a new understanding, and to "negotiate" an integration of conflicting ideas.[51]

Conclusion

Mezirow's theory of transformative learning focuses on the transformation of assumptions that govern one's thinking, feelings, and actions. These structures of assumptions are referred to as frames of reference, which have two

---

50. Mezirow, *Transformative Dimensions*; 98–99; Mezirow and Taylor, *Transformative Learning*, 19.
51. King, *Handbook of the Evolving Research*, Kindle Location, 395–398.

components: habit of mind and points of view. The habitual ways of thinking, feeling, and acting influenced by assumptions are the habits of mind. All the beliefs, values judgments, attitudes, and feelings that shape one's interpretation of experience are the points of view. Therefore, transformative learning, according to Mezirow, is a process of transforming one's frames of reference. He proposes a cognition process of reflection on conflicting experiences as a way to transform frames of reference.

Alternative Conceptions for Transformative Learning

While transformative learning, as presented by Mezirow, has been embraced by many as a viable theory for adult learning, many have criticized it for his insistence that there is no fixed truth. Mezirow says, "Learning to decide more insightfully for oneself what is right, good and beautiful is centrally concerned with bringing into awareness and negotiating one's own purposes, values, beliefs, feelings, dispositions, and judgments rather than acting on those of others."[52] While, the need to have a critical mind is valid and should be encouraged, Mezirow's overemphasis on the individual's ability to determine what is right, good, and beautiful apart from the social context and the recognition of a higher authority who determines what is of the greatest ethical and aesthetical value does not sit very well with many. He puts individuals in a state of continuous doubt of what they think they know by saying that, "Adults cannot fully trust what they know or believe because there are no fixed truths and circumstances change."[53] Gimple says that this statement is Mezirow's most problematic statement, which denies the existence of fixed truth and hence, most evangelical Christians holding to a high view of the truth and authority of Scripture may have difficulty accepting it.[54]

Habermas is one of those who has influenced Mezirow's theory of transformative learning. Pazmino, in speaking of Habermas's three categories of knowledge, says that Habermas's stance of autonomy is inadequate from a Christian perspective.[55] Ferris also picks up on that and voices his concern

---

52. Mezirow, "Epistemology," 1.
53. Mezirow, 2.
54. Gimple, "Integrating Transformative Learning," 97.
55. Pazmiño, *Foundational Issues*, 174.

regarding Mezirow's theory of transformative learning and his emphasis on an individual's ability to determine value. Ferris, Lillis, and Enlow in their analysis of Mezirow's perspective, explain that the goal of the educator in transformational education is to evoke change in perspective. They acknowledge that Mezirow's idea of perspective transformation continues to have a significant influence in the area of transformative learning. While appreciating Mezirow's contribution to transformative learning and affirming the need for altered perspective, they express their concern that within a Christian framework, Mezirow's understanding of transformation conflicts with fundamental Christian affirmations. They say,

> The appropriateness of and need for altered perspectives is very clear but the Christian needs to say much more. Unstated (but assumed) in Mezirow's writings are assumptions and values toward which Mezirow believes the learner should progress, such as value relativism and individual autonomy, grounded in a constructivist epistemology. As respected persons, the perspectives of teachers exert a significant influence on shaping the thinking of students. In academic environments, reigning perspectives often differ markedly from biblical truth and values. While perspective transformation can dramatically affect one's values and behaviors, true transformation occurs only as learner's lives align with that of Jesus Christ and the truth of God's Word.[56]

Mezirow's approach to transformative learning is also criticized for its failure to address other alternative factors that contribute to transformative learning. One of the strong criticisms has come from Taylor, who says that Mezirow's transformative learning theory has been taken as the singular approach to transformative learning. He believes that transformative learning is holistic and not only a cognitive process. He says,

> The ubiquitous acceptance of Mezirow's psychocritical view of transformative learning theory has often led to an uncontested assumption that there is a singular conception of transformative learning, overshadowing a growing presence of other theoretical

---

56. Ferris, Lillis, and Enlow, *Ministry Education*, 41.

conceptions. It will be appropriate to look at some of the ideas on the holistic nature of transformative learning.[57]

Cranton also says that the earliest critics of transformative learning theory focused on Mezirow's failure to address social change, his neglect of power issues, his disregard for the cultural context of learning, and his overemphasis on rational thought.[58] Mezirow did not consider such factors as spirituality, emotions, social relationships, and neurobiology as contributors for transformative learning.[59]

Kaisu Mälkki, for instance believes that emotions were not sufficiently valued in Mezirow's study. She says that "criticisms of the cognitive emphasis of Mezirow's theory are justifiable in the sense that the nature, role, and origins of emotions are not considered explicitly in the theory but remain rather in a subordinate role, whereas the elaboration on the cognitive aspects of learning are brought to the fore."[60] She also explains that social context plays an important role in transformative learning. In a social context where a safe and accepting atmosphere is created, learners could become less defensive and open to change.[61] John M. Dirkx and Edward W. Taylor have also written significantly on the role of emotions and the unconscious ways of transformative learning.[62]

Several of the recent literature seem to agree that transformative learning is more than a cognitive process. The following section provides a discussion of the literature on the holistic nature of transformative learning.

Transformative Learning as a Holistic Process

The discussion so far has shown that transformative learning is more than a cognitive process. It is a complex process where the physical, emotional,

---

57. Taylor, "Transformative Learning Theory," 7.
58. Cranton, *Understanding*, 43.
59. Taylor, "Transformative Learning Theory," 7.
60. Mälkki, "Building on Mezirow's," 55, quoted in Hoggan, Mälkki, and Finnegan, "Developing the Theory," 48–64.
61. Mälkki, "Theorizing the Nature," 56, quoted in Hoggan, Mälkki, and Finnegan, "Developing the Theory."
62. Dirkx, Mezirow, and Cranton, "Musings and Reflections"; Taylor, "Transformative Learning Theory."

relational, cognitive, moral, and spiritual aspects of the human person are closely intertwined. Perry Shaw suggests that "we can no longer accept the status quo of an imbalanced cognitively oriented education that is founded on the faulty epistemology of modernist objectivism."[63] Taylor adds to this by saying, "a holistic approach recognizes the role of feelings, other ways of knowing (intuition, somatic), and the role of relationships with others in the process of transformative learning."[64]

Dirkx suggests that holistic transformative learning is, "like inviting 'the whole person' into the classroom environment, we mean the person in fullness of being: as an affective, intuitive, thinking physical, spiritual self."[65] Coley and Turner, in describing how a child would respond in obedience, say that there must be "change – in perspective, attitude, knowledge, and ultimately behavior."[66] The change is not limited to cognition but includes other dimensions as well. Bernhard Ott explains the relationship between thought and action saying that thought and action are kept in relationship with one another, so that each informs, stimulates, and corrects the other.[67]

Dirkx, in a dialogue with Mezirow, asks, "How do the words of the text, of what we read, hear, see or experience become part of who we are, lend meaning to our lives, illuminate those aspects of our lives shrouded in darkness or mystery?" And he responds to his own question by saying,

> Clearly, it is more than memory, more than remembering what we read, see, hear, or experience. The process of learning represents the process of the word becoming an integral part of our being. Moreover, when this happens, it has the potential to transform our sense of self and our being in the world.[68]

He goes on to explain that such kinds of learning experiences are also "deeply emotional, evoking powerful feelings, such as fear, grief, loss, regret, and

---

63. Shaw, *Transforming Theological Education*, 77.
64. Taylor, "Transformative Learning Theory," 11.
65. Yorks and Kasl, "I Know More," 43–64, quoted in Mezirow and Taylor, *Transformative Learning*, 11.
66. Coley and Turner, *Examining Deuteronomy 6*, 6.
67. Ott, *Understanding and Developing*, 206.
68. Dirkx, Mezirow, and Cranton, "Musings and Reflections," 130.

anger, but also sometimes joy, wonder, and awe."[69] Therefore, in order to fully understand transformative learning and to be able to effectively facilitate it, the various dimensions that make up this holistic view must be explored.

Although there are varied dimensions of transformative learning mentioned in the literature, this study will focus on the three broad dimensions of learning, namely: affective, cognitive, and behavioral domains, with the hope of providing a more holistic approach to learning.

Affective Domain

This researcher has observed that new believers are made to behave in certain traditionally accepted ways. The kind of behavior that is forced is not a lasting behavior. If behavior is said to be learned, it must be a result of the person seeing the value of it and being willing to change the behavior and deciding to behave in a new way. In the same manner, one cannot assume knowledge automatically leads to a transformed behavior. The person's affect plays a significant role in experiencing transformative learning. Taylor explains that a recent study exploring the role of affective learning in transformation, found that participants could not act on cognitive learning until they had engaged in "learning how to identify, explore, validate and express affect."[70] Antonio R. Damasio says, "in the field of neurobiology, reason, which is the basis for rationality, has been traditionally perceived as a high order function. When discussing cognitive processes, emotions are often omitted, considered too illusive, despite their qualifying nature in the process of reason."[71]

James Smith, in his book *Desiring the Kingdom*, takes the discussion a step further saying that human beings are desiring, imaginative, noncognitive animals and not thinking things that are containers for ideas. Their interaction with the world is noncognitive and pre-reflective: it is an affective mode of "feeling our way around" the world. In explaining what drives decisions and actions, he explains that the ultimate desire is oriented by and to "a picture of what we think it looks like for us to live well, and that picture then governs, shapes, and motivates our decisions and actions."[72] It is not a list of

---

69. Dirkx, Mezirow, and Cranton, 132.
70. Taylor, "Transformative Learning: Neurobiological Perspective," 220.
71. Damasio, *Descartes' Error*, quoted in Taylor, "Transformative Learning: Neurobiological Perspective," 221.
72. Smith, *Desiring the Kingdom*, 53.

ideas or propositions or doctrines etc. that become motivators for decisions and actions but rather the affective, sensible, even aesthetic picture of what the good life looks like.[73]

The desire for a particular kind of a good life becomes an integral part of one's dispositions (also referred to as habits) – precognitive tendencies to act in certain ways and toward certain ends.[74] Habits govern the inclination to act in certain ways without the need to engage in reflection. This raises the question, how then are habits formed if not through the process of reflection?

Smith suggests two ways habits are inscribed into our hearts.[75] The first one is through images that are trafficked into our hearts and mind through different mediums such as stories, movies, advertisements, etc. These images, over time, begin to shape desire and fuel disposition toward them. Second, habits are inscribed into our hearts through bodily practices and rituals that train the heart, as it were, to desire certain ends. The motions and rhythms of embodied routines train the mind and heart so that habits are developed – sort of attitudinal reflexes – that make a person tend to act in certain ways toward certain ends. The point Smith makes is that decisions and actions are not all necessarily governed by cognitive reflection but more by the unconsciously developed desire which forms disposition. The center for desire is not in the mind but rather in the heart where there is no need for reflection. While Smith is not disregarding the value of cognition, he argues that its effect is significantly less than affect.[76]

Contemporary research is revealing a more integrated relationship between the physiological process of cognition and emotion. LeDoux is quoted in Taylor saying, "cognition and emotion are mediated by separate and interacting systems of the brain." Johnson-Laird and Oatley are quoted in Taylor saying, "without emotions, individuals are unable to coordinate their behavior, respond to emergencies, prioritize goals, prepare for proper action and make progress towards goals – incapable of filling the gaps often found in the slow and error-prone process of objective rationality."[77]

---

73. Smith, 53.
74. Smith, 55.
75. Smith, 58–59.
76. Smith, 53.
77. Taylor, "Transformative Learning: Neurological Perspective," 223.

These studies seem to indicate the interdependence there is between emotion and cognitive processes. Zull explains that cognitive tasks are inseparably related to emotions. He says, "reason is always driven by emotion and need. It seems unlikely that reason could ever occur without emotion."[78] A look at the brain structure indicates a connection between the amygdala, which controls emotion and the neocortex, which is the thinking, analyzing, and planning part of the brain.[79] Signals travel from the cortex to the amygdala, and vice versa. This suggests that the amygdala is set up to influence memory, ideas, plans, and judgment.[80] The brain's amygdala encodes strong emotions and bonds them to learnings for long-term storage. These emotions are found to have a higher priority than cognitive processing for commanding our attention.[81]

D. A. Sousa suggests that teachers should strive to bond positive feelings to new learnings so that students feel competent and can enjoy the process. Sousa gives us some pointers on what teachers may do to facilitate this:[82]

- Use humor (not sarcasm) as an integral part of the lesson.
- Design and tell stories that enhance understanding of the concepts. Studies show that stories engage all parts of the brain because they touch on the learner's experiences, feelings, and actions.
- Incorporate real-world examples and activities that have meaning for the learners.
- Demonstrate that they really care about their students' success. This means spending less time on the class rules and the test schedule and more time on asking, "How do you learn? What teaching strategies work best for you?"

Seeing the role of emotion (affect) as being a significant factor in transformative learning, Curzon gives us David Krathwohl's stages towards embracing a new experience. These stages of affect include.[83]

---

78. Zull, *Art of Changing*, 75.
79. Zull, 75.
80. Zull, 75.
81. Sousa, *How the Brain Learns*, 164.
82. Sousa, 164.
83. Anderson et al., *Taxonomy for Learning*, 268–69; Curzon, *Teaching in Further Education*, 165; Shaw, *Transforming Theological Education*, 71.

- Receiving – this is the stage of being willing to pay attention, consider, or receive a particular viewpoint.
- Responding – the learner goes beyond receiving it and begins to do something with the experience they had. They would engage in classroom discussions, ask questions, etc.
- Valuing – this is the stage where the learner has wrestled with the perspective and come to express a preference for a particular point of view.
- Organization – the student organizes what they value into priorities, resolving conflicts between them, and creating a unique value system (frame of reference).
- Characterization – where the students build their lives around a particular point of view and the value systems.

The teacher-student relationship is key to affective learning. In considering the example of the Lord Jesus it is clear that his primary intent was to draw men and women into a relationship with God and with one another. Varieties of studies show that genuine concern for the students and the creation of a hospitable classroom is the hallmark of exceptional teachers.[84]

In connecting the stages of affective development to that of Mezirow's transformative learning, we can see that the initial stage, in this case, is an emotional drive causing the learner's desire to listen or entertain the point of view leading to a good life. It is the emotions (desire) that move the person to the next stage. At this stage, it is possible that the learner may skip any form of reflection and begin to value what was received consciously and unconsciously, allow it to shape their habit. However, it is also possible that the learner engages in reflection through dialogue with others asking questions, and also practice, which would strengthen the desire. That leads the learner to assimilate or accommodate the new perspective and begin to determine subsequent actions (characterization).

Cognitive Domain

It is a general perception that higher educational institutions excel in the area of the cognitive domain. However, it may not be surprising that many

---

84. Ott, *Understanding and Developing*, 228; Shaw, *Transforming Theological Education*, 72.

of the higher educational institutions in Ethiopia tend to focus on the transmission of information more than anything else. This seems to be the type of education that Mezirow and Freire are both highly opposed to, teachers and others dump information into the brains of the learners, who assimilate the information without any reflection on what they are assimilating. While the reception of information is a necessary beginning to cognitive learning, it should not be the end of learning. As can be seen from the taxonomy developed by Bloom,[85] learners need to progress through the higher levels of cognitive learning. Bloom's taxonomy is given below.[86]

- Knowledge – the ability to recall facts or information.
- Comprehension – the understanding of what is being communicated, and the ability to make use of the material at a simple level.
- Application – The ability to use abstractions in particular concrete situations.
- Analysis – The ability to break material down into its constituent elements.
- Synthesis – The ability to build a structure or pattern from diverse elements or to put parts together to form a whole, creating a more comprehensive meaning or structure.
- Evaluation – The ability to make judgments about the value of ideas or materials.

Over the years, Bloom's taxonomy has been revised to place synthesis as the highest level of learning instead of evaluation.[87] Shaw also makes a suggestion that the application should be placed along with every level of learning beginning with comprehension to indicate that learners start to apply what they have learned from the time they have gained comprehension of the knowledge they have received and they continue to do so as they analyze, evaluate, and synthesize. The level of application is determined by the degree the learners are involved in reflecting on what they are learning. Shaw says,

---

85. Bloom, Englehart, Krathwohl, and Hill, *Taxonomy of Educational Objectives*, 18.
86. Anderson et al., *Taxonomy for Learning*; Curzon, *Teaching in Further Education*; Shaw, *Transforming Theological Education*.
87. Anderson et al., *Taxonomy for Learning*, 310.

"the more deeply one grasps the issues related to an idea or question, the more potentially powerful the application."[88]

A close relationship can be seen between Bloom's taxonomy and Mezirow's phases of transformative learning. Mezirow's phases of transformative learning have the following four key stages: disorienting learning experience, reflection, change of perspectives (frames of reference), and action. These can be aligned to Bloom's taxonomy. Knowledge and comprehension align with the stage that provides the disorienting experience. The learners reflect on newly gained knowledge and comprehension through the process of analysis and evaluation. Based on their reflection, they experience a change of perspectives (synthesis) and finally, they begin to act upon their new perspectives.

There are a couple of distinctions that need to be noted here. The first one is that students may have a disorienting learning experience as they gain new knowledge and comprehension. The disorienting learning experience may not be a life-shattering experience, but it may be a new knowledge or a new understanding of the knowledge they gained. A second point for us to note is that there is a possibility that one may begin to act based on a newly gained understanding without necessarily involving in reflection. An example may be a person who is taught how to greet older people in a new culture. They do not necessarily engage in critical reflection but begin to behave according to the new understanding.

Behavioral Domain

The behavioral domain deals with psychomotor skills related to the actions of the person.[89] Behavior is the outward demonstration of one's inward desire[90] or frame of reference.[91] It was the assumption, and continues to be, for many teachers that knowledge will lead learners to behave accordingly. On the contrary, Leon Festinger's research showed that the knowledge-behavior relationship works the other way around – that is, people are more likely to behave their way into thinking than think their way into behaving.[92] Shaw

---

88. Shaw, *Transforming Theological Education*, 75.
89. Newton, *Heart-Deep Teaching*, 53.
90. Smith, *Desiring the Kingdom*.
91. Mezirow, "Epistemology."
92. Festinger, *Theory of Cognitive Dissonance*, 73, quoted in Shaw, *Transforming Theological Education*.

quotes Horace Bushnell saying, "No truth is taught by words or learned by intellectual means . . . Truth must be lived into meaning before it can be truly known."[93] It is also Smith's argument that "habits are inscribed in our hearts through bodily practices and rituals that train the heart, as it were, to desire certain ends. This is a noncognitive sort of training, a kind of education that is shaping us often without our realization."[94]

Smith argues that the desire, aimed at a "good life," shapes actions and behavior. This desire for a "good life," is something that comes before thinking and hence, it is described as being precognitive. Habits (precognitive dispositions) are formed by practices – routines and rituals that inscribe particular ongoing habits in our character such that they become automatic. While some habits are acquired by choosing to engage in certain practices, many are acquired by unintentionally engaging in practices that form character. Inattention to the formative role of practices may result in inattention to all the ways such practices unintentionally form one's habits and desires. Therefore, according to Smith, the desire to behave in a certain manner or develop a certain desired skill comes from practice and it is also formed through practice.[95]

While the practice produces desire, which is precognitive, the engagement in a practice itself, involves a cognitive process. Sousa tells us that studies show that in learning a new physical skill, attention and awareness are obviously required. For this, a person uses the frontal lobe, motor cortex, and cerebellum of the brain. The frontal lobe is involved because working memory is needed, and the motor cortex of the cerebrum (a thin strip located across the top of the brain) interacts with the cerebellum to control muscle movement. A skill is therefore learned by repeatedly following a set of procedures and as the practice continues, the brain no longer needs to use its higher-order processes because the performance of the skill becomes automatic.[96]

Elizabeth J. Simpson, in her research, stated that the psychomotor domain involves cognition and motor activity, as well as affective components in the

---

93. Bushnell, *Christian Nurture*, quoted in Shaw, *Transforming Theological Education*, 73.
94. Smith, *Desiring the Kingdom*, 53.
95. Smith, 58.
96. Sousa, *How the Brain Learns*, 108.

willingness to act. In explaining the development of proficiency in a skill, she quotes Crow and Crow saying,

> The aim of motor learning is to develop proficiency in whatever skill is being learned. The simpler skills are mastered by utilizing movement already learned and combining them into a workable pattern. After the skill has been perfected to a point that the individual shows proficiency in it, he is considered to have formed the skill.[97]

She developed a schema for the classification of educational objectives in the psychomotor domain. The stages she proposes include.[98]

1. Perception – ability to use sensory cues to guide motor activity.
2. Set – readiness for a particular kind of action or experience. This has three aspects to it.
   a. Mental set – mental readiness to perform the tasks. This involves the cognitive aspect of having the necessary knowledge for the task.
   b. Physical – focusing the attention of the needed sensory organ for the task.
   c. Emotional set – attitude favorable to the action. Having the desire needed for the task.
3. Guided response – behavior under the guidance of an instructor. This is the initial stage in the learning of a complex task through imitation and trial and error.
4. Mechanism – learned response has become habitual and the action can be done with some degree of confidence and proficiency.
5. Complex overt response – an individual can perform the complex motor act. Performance is without hesitation and automatic.
6. Adaptation – performing new but related tasks based on previously used skill.
7. Origination – Creating new performances based on the understanding, abilities, and skills learned earlier.

---

97. Simpson, "Classification of Educational Objectives," 14.
98. Simpson, 21.

In her report, Simpson finishes by wondering the possibility of including adaptation and origination as possible steps following the mastery of the skill. Issler and Habermas include the elements of adaptation and origination in their summarized three-level psychomotor domain as listed below.[99]

1. Preparation – the learner is exposed to the cues and develops the mental, physical, and affective readiness to act.
2. Practice – the learner is engaged in practicing the specific behavior as it is modeled to the learner and develops in their competence and confidence to act.
3. Independent action – is not only to behave but also able to originate new behavior and actions depending on the context of the learner is.

In the development of the psychomotor domain, cognition, as well as affect, are involved. Without cognition, the learner would not know how they need to act and without the needed affective readiness, the learner would not engage in the behavior or motor action.[100] Although Simpson states that her primary focus was on skills and abilities involving some form of motor activity, she recognizes that the psychomotor domain involves behavioral actions to a considerable extent.[101]

Conclusion

In holistic transformative learning, an interaction between the three domains is observed as discussed above. No domain functions independent of the others. The behavioral domain cannot function independent of the cognition or affect. Sousa says, "when first learning the skill, attention, and awareness are obviously required,"[102] indicating the need for cognition in the development of behavior. Johnson-Laird and Oatley are also quoted in Taylor saying, "without emotions, individuals are unable to coordinate their behavior, respond to emergencies, prioritize goals, prepare for proper action and make

---

99. Issler and Habermas, *How We Learn*, quoted in Newton, *Heart-Deep Teaching*, 52–53.
100. Simpson, "Classification of Educational Objectives," 4.
101. Simpson, 7.
102. Sousa, *How the Brain Learns, 108.*

progress towards goals – incapable of filling the gaps often found in the slow and error-prone process of objective rationality."[103]

As much as behavior is influenced by cognition and affect, cognition is also influenced by behavior and affect. As Johnson-Laird and Oatley said above, it is not possible to progress towards achieving goals or preparing a plan of action without emotions. The cognition, therefore, functions in interaction with emotion. Zull also explains that cognitive tasks are inseparably related to emotions. He says, "reason is always driven by emotion and need. It seems unlikely that reason could ever occur without emotion."[104] With the increased practice of a certain behavior, cognition is also improved.

Affect is also influenced by both cognition and behavior. As one gains knowledge and begins to understand, the person's emotions are influenced in one way or another. Affect is also influenced by practice. As Smith says, emotions are developed "through bodily practices and rituals that train the heart, as it were, to desire certain ends. The motions and rhythms of embodied routines train our minds and heart so that we develop habits."[105]

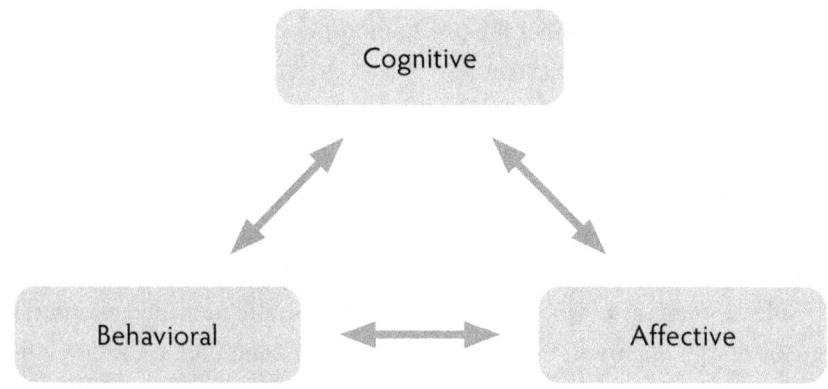

Figure 3: Concerted functioning of the learning domains

As it is illustrated in figure 3, a degree of development in cognition will influence desire (affect) and also behavior or psychomotor skill. An increased degree of affect will also have an influence on the cognitive growth as well

---

103. Taylor, "Transformative Learning: Neurobiological Perspective," 223.
104. Zull, *Art of Changing*, 73.
105. Smith, *Desiring the Kingdom*, 53.

as the mastery of a certain desired behavior. An increased level of performance in behavior will influence the development of cognition and it also shapes affect.

The discussion on the three domains so far shows that they all aim at training the learner to demonstrate competency related to either behavior or mastery of a certain action. In the affective domain, it is expected that the learner would begin to value what has been accepted and climax with characterization. In the cognitive domain, the learner begins to comprehend, analyze, evaluate, and through all the stages, the learner experiences a transformed frame of mind and engages in applying this in real life. In the behavioral domain, as a result of a transformed frame of mind and attitude to act in a set manner, followed with practice, the behavior becomes habituated and automatic.

All of the three domains seem to progressively go through the process of interacting with each other and working towards achieving a similar goal of forming character and skill. In that process of interaction between the different domains, the learner continues to undergo a transformation in the cognitive frame of reference, desire, as well as the degree of behavioral competence.

Therefore, holistic transformative learning may be perceived as a change in one's cognitive frame of reference, affect (desire), and psychomotor domains resulting in the desired outcome of behavioral and skill formation which reflects an integration of the three domains.

Theories of Adult Learning

So far, Mezirow's understanding of transformative learning and alternative theories including the holistic approach to transformative learning have been discussed. In the following section, three different perspectives on adult learning will be presented. These perspectives include brain science in relation to learning, experiential learning by David Kolb, and Duane Elmer's learning cycle.

Brain Science and Learning

Until recently, the physical processes going on in the brain could only be guessed at based on the output (action or reaction) of an individual. The recent advances in medical technology have made it possible for scientists to observe the brain at work. This section provides an overview of the brain structure and its functions as it relates to learning. Understanding concepts related to brain structure and the general activities will help gain a clear picture of the three learning theories discussed in this section.

The cerebral cortex, which is responsible for much of the thinking and learning, has three highly generalized functions – namely, sensing, integrating, and action. The brain receives information through the different senses and the sensory information is then integrated as a whole producing ideas and plans for action that are then executed by the motor cortex.[106]

The backside of the cerebral cortex functions in receiving, remembering, and integrating information that comes from outside and within the body itself. There are three lobes in this section that carry out these functions. The parietal lobe integrates information from various parts of the body. The visual information is processed through the occipital lobes. The temporal lobes deal with sound, music, and face and object recognition. The temporal lobes also deal with processing all the information and partly also with long-term memory. Therefore, in this part of the brain, sensory information is brought in and integrated through the process of assimilation (producing meaning as signals are added to existing concepts, which Piaget refers to as assimilation) or combined into new units that expand conceptual understanding (which Piaget refers to as accommodation).[107]

The front side of the cerebral cortex functions in modifying, creating, and controlling. The frontal lobe and the motor cortex are found in this section of the brain too and carry out these tasks. The frontal lobe comprises the rational and executive control center of the brain, integrating the information, planning and making choices, decisions to act, inhibition, and emotions associated with the action.[108] The motor cortex coordinates the learning of the motor skills engaging in action.

Besides these major parts of the brain that are engaged in sensing, integrating, and acting, the limbic system is also responsible for several functions of the brain. Sousa explains that the limbic system can no longer be viewed as

---

106. Zull, *Art of Changing*; Sousa, *How the Brain Learns*.

107. Ferris, Lillis, and Enlow, *Ministry Education*; Zull, *Art of Changing*; Sousa, *How the Brain Learns*.

108. Zull, *Art of Changing*; Sousa, *How the Brain Learns*.

being a separate entity. The limbic system has structures that have functions that include generating emotions and processing emotional memories. These structures are found duplicated in each of the hemispheres of the brain. The limbic system has four parts: the thalamus, hypothalamus, hippocampus, and amygdala. The thalamus is where all outside information (except for smell) goes first, before being directed to the other parts of the brain. Signals from the cerebrum and cerebellum also come to the thalamus involving it in cognitive activities including memory. The hypothalamus monitors the internal systems maintaining a balance by releasing a variety of hormones, as necessary. The hippocampus consolidates learning and converts information from working memory to long-term storage regions. It checks information relayed to working memory and compares it to stored experiences. This process is essential for the creation of meaning. It helps in the recall of facts, objects, and places. It is capable of producing new neurons, (a process called) neurogenesis. Finally, the amygdala plays an important role in emotions, especially fear. The emotional component of memory is believed to be stored here and it is recalled whenever the particular memory is recalled. The interaction between the hippocampus and the amygdala ensures that one would remember for a long time those events that are important and emotional.[109] As can be seen in the following section, David Kolb's experiential learning theory has a close relationship with how the human brain learns. A brief discussion of Kolb's theory of learning is presented here.

Experiential Learning Theory – David Kolb

Experiential learning theory is described as a "holistic integrative perspective on learning that combines experience, perception, cognition, and behavior." As opposed to the cognitive theory, its focus goes beyond just the acquisition, manipulation, and recall of abstract symbols. It is also different from the behavioral learning theory which denies any role of the cognition and subjective experiences in the learning process.[110]

The experiential learning theory is derived from the theories put forward by Dewey, Lewin, and Piaget. Kolb gives us a brief description of the theories of the four as follows.

---
109. Sousa, *How the Brain Learns*, 20.
110. Kolb, *Experiential Learning*, 63.

Lewin's model of experiential learning.

In Lewin's theory of the action research and laboratory method,[111] transformation is perceived to happen by an integrated process that begins with the learner's here-and-now experience, followed by the collection of data and observation about that experience (see figure 4). Based on the analysis and conclusions of the data, the learner forms possible hypotheses or generalizations, which the learner then tests in new situations.

There are two aspects that are significant in this process. The first one is that it is focused on the immediate testing of a hypothesis. The second aspect is that it is based on a feedback process. The hypothesis is implemented in a new situation and the data are again collected and analyzed confirming or modifying the previous experience.

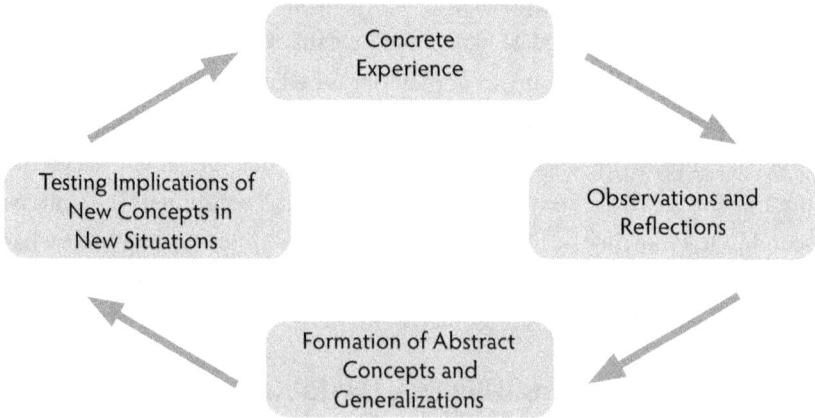

Figure 4: The Lewinian experiential learning model[112]

Dewey's model of experiential learning.

Dewey's model of experiential learning focusses on the transformation of impulses, feelings, and desires, which are derived from concrete experiences, into purposeful action. Actions implemented based on an impulse are blind

---

111. Kolb, 63.
112. Kolb, 63.

actions. However, purposeful actions are those that the learner, who has had an experience, is engaged in:[113]

- Observation of the conditions surrounding the experience
- Knowledge of what happened in the past through recollection and information, advice, and warning gathered from those who have had wider experience
- Judgment/formation of conclusions by combining observation and knowledge
- Develop a purposeful plan of action (foresight)
- Purposeful action

Foresight is necessary to guide purposeful action. However, Dewey says,

> Mere foresight, even if it takes the form of accurate prediction, is not, of course, enough. The intellectual anticipation, the idea of consequences, must blend with desire and impulse to acquire moving force. It then gives direction to what otherwise is blind, while desire gives ideas impetus and momentum.[114]

Jean Piaget's model of learning.

Kolb states that experience and concept and reflection and action are on a continuum for developing adult thought. Learning happens through the process of assimilation and accommodation. He describes learning in the words of Piaget saying that "the key to learning lies in the mutual interaction of the process of accommodation of concepts or schemas to experience in the world and the process of assimilation of events and experiences from the world into existing concepts and schemas."[115] The process of cognitive growth from concrete to abstract and from active to reflective is based on this continual transaction between assimilation and accommodation, occurring in successive stages, each of which incorporates what has gone before into a new, higher level of cognitive functioning.[116]

---

113. Kolb, 64.
114. Kolb, 64.
115. Kolb, 65.
116. Kolb, 65.

Kolb sees a great deal of similarity between these three models of learning from which his model of experiential learning is developed. His perspective on learning, which is drawn from concepts discussed in the three models, can be described using the following propositions.[117]

1. Learning is best conceived as a process, not as an outcome. Ideas are believed to be formed and re-formed through experience rather than remaining fixed and immutable. Therefore, concepts are derived from and continuously modified by experience. The definition of learning in terms of outcomes is considered to be a definition of non-learning. Paulo Freire calls the learning process that is based on the transmission of fixed concepts as the "banking" education where the learner is the depositories, and the teacher is the depositor.[118]
2. Learning is a continuous process grounded in experience – knowledge is continuously derived from and tested out in the experiences of the learner. Learning is re-learning. The importance of recognizing that all learners have a certain level of knowledge on topics that are discussed in class is stressed. Learning should be not only introducing new concepts but also removing old concepts students have held regarding the topic. The learning process should then seek to bring out the existing understanding, test the existing understanding, and then integrate the new more refined understanding into the learner's belief system.[119]
3. Learning is a holistic process of adaptation to the world. Learning is not related only to cognition or behavior of the learner but rather it is related to the complete function of the learner – thinking, feeling, perceiving, and behaving.[120]

---

117. Kolb, 67–74.
118. Kolb, 67.
119. Kolb, 68.
120. Kolb, 74.

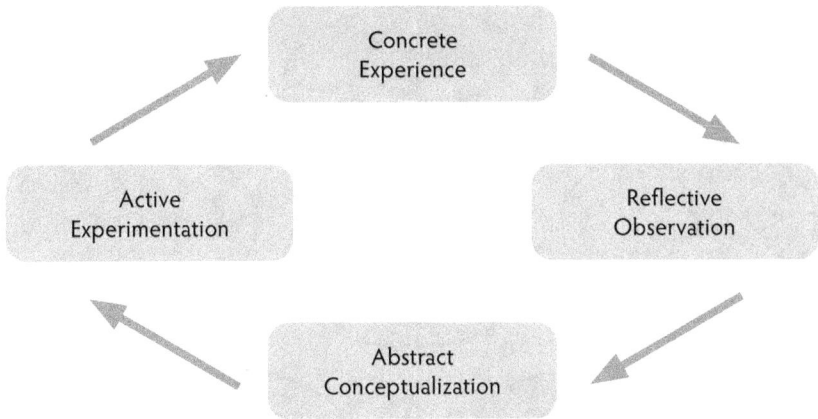

Figure 5: Kolb's experiential learning[121]

According to Kolb, as figure 5 shows, learning begins with concrete experience that may be physical, aural, visual (from the environment), or verbal (through conversation or reading). The entry points are the five sense organs. The next step in the process is reflective observation. It involves organizing sensory data, attempting to make meaning from it, and locating it with respect to prior experience. At this point, understanding of what was experienced occurs. As learning progresses and a person reflects on the meaning of experiences, the person begins to explore its implications. They then build abstract hypotheses about the way this bit of understanding may relate to the rest of what the person "knows," and they then plan ways to use or test their understanding. The final step is the active experimentation where a person may take many different forms such as expressing it to others for them to dispute if needed and using it in real life situations.[122]

Elmer's Cycle of Learning

Duane and Muriel Elmer have proposed the cycle of learning based on Kolb's learning cycle. This researcher has found this cycle to be insightful in understanding the process of learning. The cycle is presented in figure 6.

---

121. Kolb, 83.
122. Ferris, Lillis, and Enlow, *Ministry Education*, 36–37.

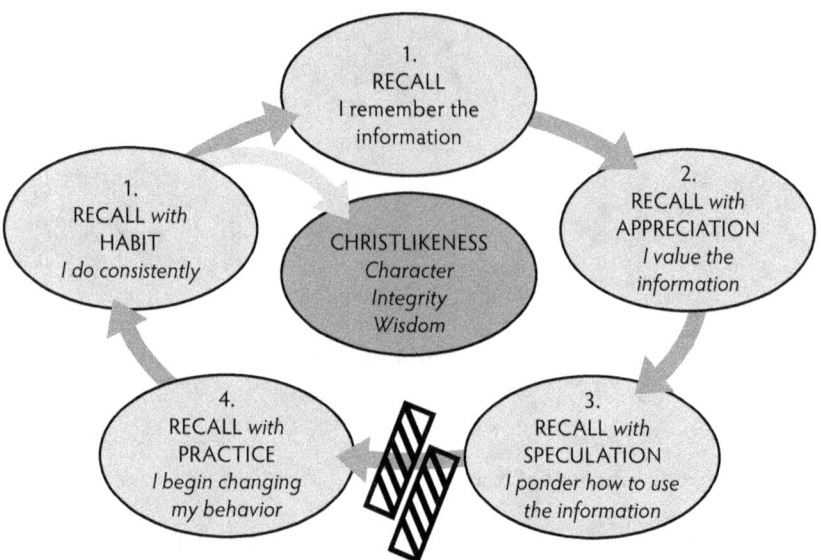

Figure 6: Elmer's cycle of learning.[123] Since the completion of this work, Muriel and Duane Elmer have published a book on the learning cycle[124]

In Elmer's learning cycle, learning begins by mastering the necessary information needed for transformation. The student will learn to develop certain skills when they have first mastered the facts about the particular skill. Ferris says that this is especially true in theological colleges where the mastery of the biblical truth should take precedence prior to requiring students to behave in certain manners.[125] Psalm 119:11 seems to support this as well where it says, "I have hidden your word in my heart that I may not sin against you" (NIV).

The next level in the cycle is an emphasis on appreciation. The content the students are receiving must be valued in order for it to be of any use to them. Ferris explains the role of this stage to learning by saying,

> When students leave our classroom with feelings of boredom, apathy, or frustration, the significance of the truth we teach may be lost. It is unlikely they will value that truth or do anything

---

123. Diagram from *The Learning Cycle: Insights for Faithful Teaching from Neuroscience and the Social Sciences*, by Muriel I. Elmer and Duane H. Elmer, IVP Academic, 2020. Used with permission.

124. Elmer and Elmer, *Learning Cycle*, Kindle Edition, ch. 1.

125. Ferris, Lillis, and Enlow, *Ministry Education*, 56.

more with it. When they leave with feelings of interest, excitement, and appreciation, however, they are stimulated to pursue that truth, to reflect on it, and to obey it, even to share it with others.[126]

This stage is parallel to Kolb's second step of reflection in his learning cycle. Therefore, the element of valuing and reflection go hand in hand at this stage of Elmer's learning cycle. Instructors desire for the students to reflect on what they are experiencing. However, they will reflect on the things that they value. The value students put on their experiences is determined by their classroom experience, the information shared in the classroom, and their interaction with the teacher. Where students are placing a positive value on what they are learning, they will be able to examine their previously held ideas, assumptions, and practices.

In the third level, students begin to speculate by considering how they may apply in their life and ministry what they have valued in the previous stage. Students will consider the changes they need to make as a result of what they have found out and how they would be able to make those changes in their lives. This would be in line with Kolb's third stage of abstract conceptualization. The last three stages of the cycle are where the student applies and integrates into life and ministry the things that are learned. This stage may parallel Kolb's last stage where the student is testing the new experience.

Theoretical Framework

The discussions on transformative learning and the different perspectives on adult learning have led the researcher to consider the following transformative learning framework to guide this research. There are two key elements to observe in this framework.

Transformative Learning as a Cyclical Process

Transformative learning follows a cyclical process that is drawn from the combination of David Kolb's experiential learning cycle, Mezirow's phases

---

126. Ferris, Lillis, and Enlow, 56.

of transformative learning, and Muriel and Duane Elmer's learning cycle as shown in figure 7.

Jack Mezirow	David Kolb	Duane Elmer
1. Disorienting dilemma	Concrete experience	Recall
2. Self-examination with a feeling of guilt or shame	Reflective observation	Recall with appreciation
3. Critical assessment of epistemic, sociocultural, or psychic assumptions		Barriers
4. Recognize others go through a similar change		
5. Explore options for new roles, relationships, and actions	Abstract hypothesis	Recall with speculation
6. Plan a new course of action		
7. Acquire knowledge and skill for action	Active testing	Recall with application
8. Try the new role		
9. Build competence in the new role		
10. Integrate into habit		Recall with integration
		Christlikeness

Figure 7: Select adult learning theories comparison chart

From figure 7, five key stages can be identified that are significant to a transformative learning experience as shown in figure 8, which closely follow the components of Elmer's cycle.

First, the learning experience. The experience may be a disorienting dilemma as Mezirow suggests but it can also be the physical, aural, or visual stimulus, from the environment, or verbal input, through conversation or reading. The entry point to the learning experiences is the five sense organs: eyes, ears, nose, mouth, and skin.[127] Meaningful learning experiences are those that create tension to gain the learner's attention. Making students aware of the need to know what is about to be taught is a significant means of creating proper tension.[128]

---

127. Ferris, Lillis, and Enlow, *Ministry Education*, 38.
128. Graham, *Teaching Redemptively*, 167.

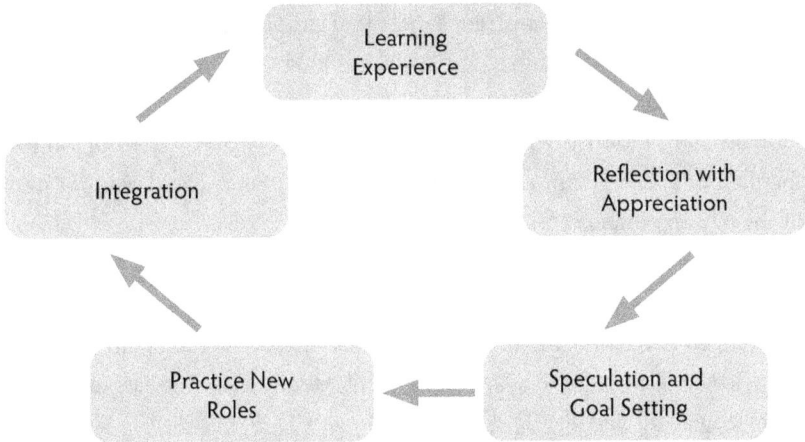

Figure 8: Transformative learning process (combining Mezirow, Kolb, and Elmer)

Second, reflection with appreciation. This is to organize sensory data, attempt to make meaning from it, and locate it with respect to prior experience. Oppewal is quoted in Graham referring to this stage as the "consider" phase of learning. In this phase, learners may choose to follow any of the following three courses: (1) retreat from the situation, perhaps denying much of what they are experiencing, (2) attack the situation in order to master it, perhaps still unable to cope comfortably with what is happening, or (3) assess what is happening and reorganize their beliefs and perceptions to develop new insights to direct their behavior.[129]

The experiences learners have may be perceived as irrelevant, consonant, or dissonant in relation to their existing beliefs and perceptions. In the case where the experience is irrelevant, the learners retreat from it. If the experience is consonant to their existing beliefs and perceptions, it will strengthen the existing behavior and beliefs but would likely not produce a new behavior. In the case where there is dissonance, the learners would experience creative tension and it is likely to cause a reorganization of the existing belief and perceptions resulting in new behavior.[130]

---

129. Donald Oppewal, "Biblical Knowing and Classroom Methodology," quoted in Graham, *Teaching Redemptively*, 168.

130. Festinger, *Theory of Cognitive Dissonance*, quoted in Graham, *Teaching Redemptively*, 173.

Third, in speculation/abstract conceptualization the learner would begin to speculate what can change. The desire gained in the previous stage would give the impetus to plan and set a possible goal for change.

Fourth, in practice/active experimentation the learner attempts to test the plan of action. With repeated practice, the learner would gain mastery of the new experience.

Fifth, integration, at this stage the learner has formed a new habit where the action automatically results from a concerted transformation in cognition, affect, and behavior. The learner is now set not only to exhibit the new behavior but also begin to adapt to new contexts and also originate new skills, knowledge, and desire.

These five stages in the learning cycle are combined into three broad steps that happen in transformative learning:

1. Becoming aware of a need to change. This first one is where the learner has an "aha" moment – the learner has an experience, and the experience causes the learner to recognize that something needs to change.
2. Reflective practice. The second step is where the learner engages in the analysis and evaluation of possible alternatives as guided by the newly discovered desire and begins to act to try out the new behavior, point of view, or skill.
3. Integrative generation. In the third step, the learner's values are changed, skills become automatic, and the learner begins to behave in a new way. It is also evidenced by the learner's ability to generate new ideas and ways of doing things.

These three stages are supported by Ott's suggestion for possible areas of development.[131] These are:

- Awareness of one's own character and intentional effort to change in those areas that are deficient.
- Recognition of one's own gifts and potential.
- Mastery of the growth steps necessary in each phase of life.

---

131. Ott, *Understanding and Developing*, 227.

Transformative Learning as a Holistic Process

Transformative learning is holistic involving cognition, affect, and behavior. When these work in concert, they form a person's disposition.[132] A transformation of a person's disposition (their cognitive frame of reference, deep desire reflected in character, and degree of behavioral competence), follows the phases in the transformative learning cycle shown above. The taxonomies proposed for each of the three domains work in concert at different stages of the transformative learning cycle building towards its integration. Figure 9 shows how each of the taxonomies relates to the stages in the transformative learning process.

Constructs	Stages of Transformative Learning	Affective	Cognitive	Behavioral
Awareness of Need	Experience Reflection	Receiving Responding	Knowledge Comprehension	Perception Set (mental, physical, emotional)
Reflective Practice	Speculation Practice	Valuing	Analysis Evaluation	Guided response Mechanism Complex overt response
Integrative Generation	Integrative generation	Organization Characterization	Application Synthesis	Adaptation Origination
Resulting Outcomes		Deep change characterization	Changed cognitive frame of reference	Skill formation

Figure 9: Constructs, transformative learning stages, and learning taxonomies

Transformative learning, therefore, happens as an integrated process where the learner progresses through the different elements of disposition

---

132. Shaw, *Transforming Theological Education*, 76.

(cognitive, affect, and behavior) within the transformative learning cycle, as shown in figure 10.

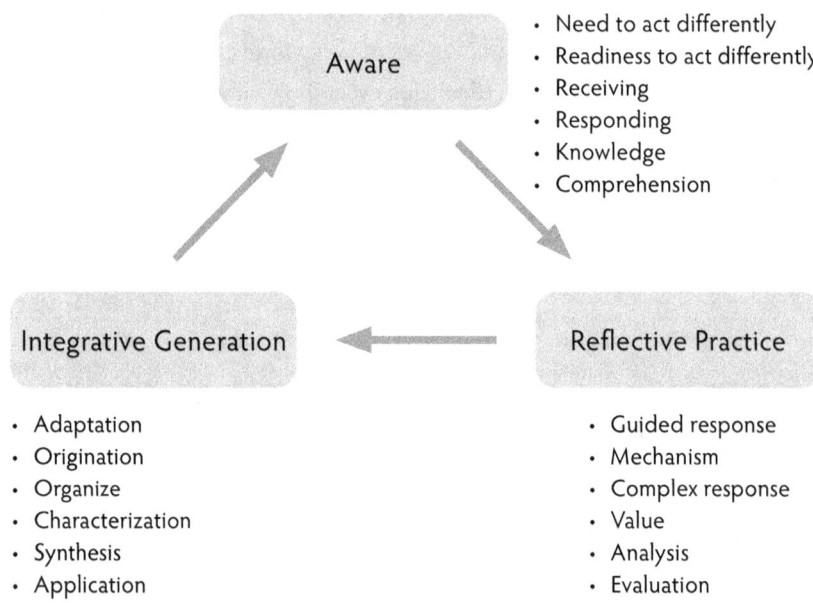

Figure 10. Transformative learning constructs

At each of the stages, the elements of disposition (cognition, affect, and behavior) work in concert moving the transformative learning process forward, as shown in figure 11.

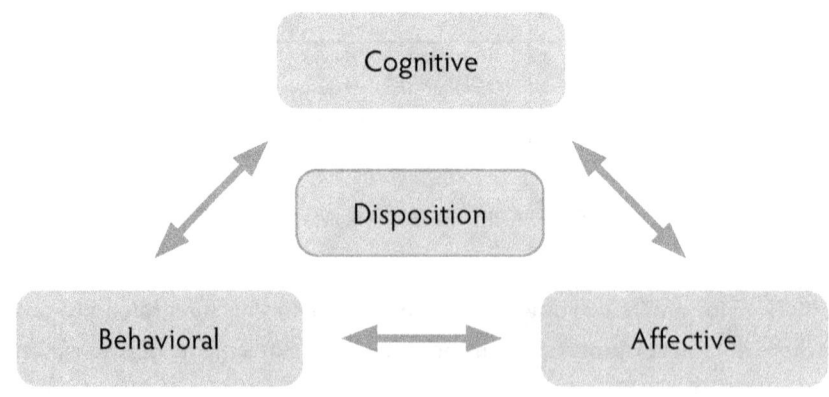

Figure 11. Concerted interaction of learning domains

Instructional Strategies for Transformative Learning

In the review of the theological perspective on education, it was said that learners are not mere "heads" to unlatch, open up, and pour content into; imparting knowledge is not enough. Education must be one that involves the appropriation, development, and expression of sanctified thoughts, emotions, decisions, actions, motivations, and purposes.[133] Such kinds of teaching will require the active engagement of the learners, differentiated instruction, and participation in a supportive group submitted to the work of the Holy Spirit.

Students, as God's image-bearers, come with a reservoir of experience and are capable of reasoning. The teacher does not need to present themself as the redeemer while the students are perceived to be completely lost. This means, that the teacher and the students can have a dialogue within a classroom. Paulo Freire describes the lack of this dialogue in the classroom by comparing the teacher-student relationship to the relationship between a slave and the master, where dialogue is not possible.[134] However, it should not be so in the classrooms if one is to see a transformation. Freire says,

> The important thing is to help me (and nations) help themselves, to place them in consciously critical confrontation with their problems, to make them the agents of their own recuperation. In contrast, assistencialism robs men of a fundamental human necessity – responsibility.[135]

Students learn as they are actively engaged in their own learning process. The relationship between the teacher and student must be "I-thou relationship, and thus necessarily a relationship between two subjects. Each time the 'thou' is changed into an object, an 'it,' dialogue is subverted, and education is changed to deformation."[136] This does not mean there is no place for the teacher to give instruction or that the teacher is not more knowledgeable than the student is, but rather it is to say that the student is equally made in the image of God with the capacity for rational thinking and hence with

---

133. Allison, "Humanity, Sin."
134. Freire, *Pedagogy of the Oppressed*, 45.
135. Freire, *Education for Critical Consciousness*, 12.
136. Freire, 45.

proper guidance, the student can be made an active participant in their own learning. Wiggins and McTighe explain an engaging instructional design as:

> That which the diverse learners find truly thought provoking, fascinating, energizing. It pulls them all deeper into the subject and they have to engage by the nature of the demands, mystery, or challenge into which they are thrown. The goal is to affect them on many levels; it must not be dry academic content, but interesting and relevant work, intellectually compelling and meaningful. Learners should not merely enjoy the work; it should engage each of them in worthy intellectual effort, centered on big ideas and important performance challenges.[137]

After an eight-day training for educators at a seminary in Cuba, Coley did a study on the use of active instructional strategies and he concluded that the educators embraced the concepts of engagement, reflective practice, and metacognitive discussions. The participants expressed a strong interest in making use of differentiated instruction, active learning techniques, and formative assessments.[138]

Teaching that engages the students is also modeled in Jesus's teaching ministry. Coley quotes a professor at Shalom University in the Democratic Republic of Congo, who identifies Jesus as the best example of an engaging teacher.

> Modern research into the human brain suggests that educational approaches similar to Jesus's informal, questioning, challenging approach are the most effective for bringing about real learning. When students remain passive in a programme of study, simply listening or reading with little interaction, then serious learning is much less likely to take place, and most of what is taught are quickly forgotten. It is when they are engaged – asking and answering questions, discussing issues and arguing a case – that their brain cells fire into life . . . In the course of Jesus's teaching, he engaged his disciples actively and thus fostered profound and long-term learning including the capacity to reason biblically

---

137. Wiggins and McTighe, *Understanding by Design*, 195.
138. Coley, "How Would It Play," 427.

and theologically. Moreover, learning is more likely to take place when people see the relevance of what is taught . . . Given that Jesus's teaching took place in response to the real situations he faced, the disciples could immediately recognize its relevance.[139]

A number of studies done on predictive factors for transformative learning confirm that college-related learning assignments significantly predict or explain perceived transformative learning experiences.[140]

Transformative instructional strategies also require students being placed in a supportive relationship with one another. As a body of believers who have come together to learn and be equipped for ministry, each learner has a reservoir of experience and spiritual gifting that can be used for building up others in the group. Boyd and Myers are quoted in Cranton emphasizing the supportive role of others saying that the learning group as a social system, "can provide supportive structures that facilitate an individual's work in realizing personal transformation."[141] Cranton suggests the following strategies for creating supporting groups:[142]

- Using small group activities or discussions during which learners can get to know each other and develop alliances.
- Forming project groups or teams in which people work together over a longer period in an area of common interest.
- Encouraging study partnerships or groups either informally or by setting up such groups as a part of the program.
- Using peer teaching (participants sharing expertise with each other), jigsaw activities (each student or small group acquires expertise on one topic and then shares it with others), buzz groups (where students join together in small groups to address specific questions), or any other techniques for bringing people together.

---

139. Coley, 428.

140. Gerke, "Learning Experiences"; King, *Handbook of Evolving Research*; Madsen and Cook, "Transformative Learning."

141. Boyd and Myers, "Transformative Education," 261–84, quoted in Cranton, *Understanding*, 163.

142. Cranton, *Understanding*, 167.

There is a dominant perception that all learners have similar needs and learn similarly, "one-size-fits-all," and hence education is not differentiated among the learners.

Dosch and Zidon say that there is a "mismatch between college instruction and students' academic needs. In addition, the current educational system works hard to keep the traditional ideals and 'one-size-fits-all' methods in place rather than employing more learner-centered approaches."[143] There are several studies of instructional differentiation done at the K-12 level. The studies done at the college level seem to be relatively fewer due to the typically large class size, the minimal number of contact hours with students, and designing several strategies is time-consuming. However, Dosch and Zidon report that there were a few of the studies that reported better achievement of goals and student satisfaction in learning. However, a few of the other experimental studies showed that there was no significant difference between the experimental group and the control group.[144]

Cranton argues that learners are all individuals with important differences. She attempts to explain that learners are different in many ways and hence they also experience transformative learning differently. She argues saying,

> The adult education literature contains many ways of classifying and explaining individual differences. Developmental phase, learning style, multiple intelligences, personality type, cognitive style, past experience, and self-directed learning readiness are just some of the ways in which writers try to account for learners' behavior and to predict how they will behave in the future. Many of these attempts to classify learners lead to dichotomies or mutually exclusive categories. People are described as visual learners or auditory learners; they are in the leaving-home phase or the moving-into-the-adult-world phase.[145]

Tomlinson and Allan also explain the diversity of the learners and the need to diversify the instructional strategies used in the classrooms.

---

143. Dosch and Zidon, "Course Fits Us," 343.
144. Dosch and Zidon, 345–46.
145. Cranton, *Understanding*, 79.

A teacher who is comfortable and skilled with the use of multiple instructional strategies is more likely to reach out effectively to varied students than is the teacher who uses a single approach to teaching and learning. Teachers are particularly limited when the sole or primary instructional strategy is teacher-centered (such as lecture), or drill-and-practice (such as worksheets).[146]

Differentiated learning instructions may involve providing a diversity of learning options and instructional strategies that may be auditory, visual, or kinesthetic.[147] In order to develop instructional strategies appropriate to a diversity of learning, it will be helpful to understand the learners' readiness, interest, and learning profiles (how students learn).[148] The thing that needs to be differentiated in deciding on instructional strategies may include the content, process, and product. The content is what the students are expected to learn. The process is the skills students employ to make sense of what they are learning. The product is that which allows the students to demonstrate and extend what they have learned.[149]

Therefore, the varieties and complexities of the learners demand a study of the learners. Failure to do that may likely result in failure of teaching for many if not for all students.[150] It would then be right to conclude that "different people engage in transformative learning in different ways."[151]

There are different methodologies of teaching that are used in higher education, but space would allow us to briefly describe only a few of them. Ellington broadly groups instructional strategies into mass-instructional methods, individualized methods, and group learning methods. The mass instructional methods primarily focus on the teacher and they include such methods as lectures and demonstrations. The individualized methods primarily focus on the learners and they include methods such as research, presentation, homework, note-taking, etc. The group learning methods are focused on the learners working together. It depends on the contributions of each

---

146. Tomlinson and Allan, *Leadership for Differentiating*, 11.
147. Tomlinson and Allan, 10.
148. Tomlinson and Imbeau, *Leading and Managing*, 18.
149. Tomlinson, *Differentiated Classroom*, 11.
150. Tomlinson and McTighe, *Integrating Differentiated Instruction*, 12.
151. Cranton, *Understanding*, 43.

member of the groups. Some of the methods here include buzz groups, class discussions, case studies, group projects, etc.[152] Of the different instructional strategies that are available for a teacher to use, the ones that will be described here will be the ones that are likely to be used within the Ethiopian context.

Mass Instructional Strategies

Mass instructional strategies are those methods that primarily center on the active engagement of the teacher. The students are, for the most part, passive in the process. Two of the mass instructional strategies that will be looked at here are lectures and demonstrations.

Lecture method

The lecture method is the process of delivering a body of knowledge to students. It is integral to learning as one way of offering new input. Jane Vella quotes Bloom to show that lecture has been overemphasized out of proportion and hence heavily criticized – "Because of the simplicity of teaching and evaluating knowledge, it [lecture] is frequently emphasized as an educational objective out of all proportion to its usefulness or its relevance for the development of the individual."[153] Despite the many criticisms of the lecture method, when carefully planned and skillfully delivered, it gives a pleasurable experience to the teachers by allowing them to cover the content they would like to cover. The students also find it to be pleasurable as it enhances understanding and generates interest.[154]

Barth is quoted in Shaw giving us a different perspective on lecture method as follows:

> Lecturing is an unnatural act, an act for which Providence did not design humans. It is perfectly all right now and then to speak while others remain silent, but to do so regularly, one hour at a time, for one person to drone on and on while others sit in

---

152. Ellington, *How Students Learn*, 109–10, quoted in Biadgelign Ademe Mekonnen, *General Learning-Teaching Methods*, 109–10.
153. Vella, *Taking Learning to Task*, 18.
154. Mekonnen, *General Learning-Teaching Methods*, 113.

silence, I do not believe that this is what the Creator designed humans to do.[155]

There is a place for lecturing in transformative learning. However, the danger is when its focus becomes the teaching of information rather than learning. When it is focused on what the teacher does instead of what the student is doing, it has gone off its purpose. The student would not be required to respond in any way and dependency and passivity would be promoted. It is suggested that lecture is most helpful when used as an introduction to the field, to provide a detailed description of a key system or process and is followed by whole-class or small group discussion of the material.[156] Bligh says that lecture method should be used relatively sparingly and that "it behooves lecturers to lecture less . . . and create opportunities, in lessons and outside in which thinking can flourish."[157] The lecture method in the hands of effective instructors can be described as that which is used to clarify and simplify complex material or to inspire attention to important matters. It should not be used as a means to cover some subject, or "as a way to impress students with how much the teacher knows."[158] Bain concludes his discussion on lecture saying that in the hands of effective teachers the "lecture was a part of a larger quest, one element of a learning environment rather than the entire experience."[159]

Stephen Brookfield gives three important qualities in preparing a good lecture.

First, they use a variety of teaching and communication approaches. Some of the ideas for doing this are described in Brookfield[160] as follows:

a. Deliberate introduction of periods of silence during which students would think and respond to reflective questions related to the material presented.

---

155. Barth, *Learning by Heart*, 34–35, quoted in Shaw, *Transforming Theological Education*, 183.

156. Shaw, *Transforming Theological Education*; Mekonnen, *General Learning-Teaching Methods*.

157. Bligh, *What's the Use*, 182, quoted in Brookfield, *Skillful Teacher*, 100.

158. Bain, *Best College Teachers Do*, 107.

159. Bain, 107.

160. Brookfield, *Skillful Teacher*, 102–5.

b. Introduce buzz groups into lectures – the buzz groups get two or three students to work together on a question or a task set for two or three minutes and report their conclusions to the class.
c. Calculated movement – there are areas of the classroom where students may remain unnoticed. The lecturer moves to those places and lectures from there to ensure that all students are included.
d. Break lectures into ten- to fifteen-minute "chunks" – Bligh says that the optimum attention span is twelve minutes. In order to keep the students engaged, he suggests that the lecture is chunked into fifteen-minute expositions interspersed with a number of linking activities.[161]

Second, lectures are clearly organized so students can follow the lecturer's train of thought. There are two ways this can be done as described by Brookfield.[162]

a. Scaffolding notes – this is a summary of the lecture that includes the main and sub-points of the lecture. It helps the students to follow the lecture. It should not include so much that the students do not need to be taking notes.
b. Give clear verbal signals – these are important to help the students recognize that an important point is being made or the direction of the lecture is changing.

Third, teachers model learning behavior – this is done by posing questions at the beginning of the lecture, raising questions from the lecture, and pointing out any question that may not have been answered by the lecture, present different perspectives on the topic and also by encouraging students to assess their assumptions that inform their ideas and actions.[163]

Demonstration

The demonstration method is one of the mass instructional methods that combines telling, showing, and doing, so as to facilitate the understanding

---

161. Bligh, *What's the Use*, quoted in Brookfield, *Skillful Teacher*, 106.
162. Brookfield, *Skillful Teacher*, 106–9.
163. Brookfield, 109–12.

level of students.[164] The intent of a demonstration is to help learners understand the concept but also to enable them to do it on their own. Therefore, although the teacher performs demonstrations, they are followed by the students practicing it.[165] Curzon reminds us that students must be prepared for the demonstration by receiving the necessary preliminary knowledge regarding the concept to be demonstrated and be tested on it prior to the demonstration. In the process of demonstration, the teacher should provide an account of the pattern of events as they unfold.[166] Demonstrations are great instructional strategies when teaching a skill or explain complex topics.[167]

Individualized Instructional Strategies

Individualized instructional strategies are those methods that primarily center on the active engagement of the students on their own learning. The students are active in the learning process. Some of the common methods in this section include summarizing, note-taking, homework, inquiry method, reading quiz and examination, and in-class presentations. Each one of them will be briefly discussed.

Summarizing

The process of summarizing a given reading engages the students in a careful reading of a text and requires them to do a certain level of analysis of their reading in formulating its main idea. Marzano gives us three generalizations based on research done by Valerie Anderson and Suzanne Hidi on summarizing.[168] The generalizations are:

1. In summarizing students are engaged in deleting some information, substituting some information, and keep some information.
2. In order to delete, substitute and keep the information, it requires the students to do a fair amount of analysis of the information

---

164. Mekonnen, *General Learning-Teaching Methods*, 148.
165. Mekonnen, 148.
166. Curzon, *Teaching in Further Education*, 284.
167. Mekonnen, *General Learning-Teaching Methods*.
168. Anderson and Hidi, "Teaching Students to Summarize," 26–28, quoted in Marzano, Pickering, and Pollock, *Classroom Instruction*, 30–32.

to be summarized. Strategies that emphasize the analytic aspect of summarizing, produces the most powerful effects in terms of students' ability to summarize.
3. Being aware of the explicit structure of the information is an aid to summarizing the information.

Note-taking

This is closely related to summarizing as it requires the students to listen to the instructor and determine what is most important and then state that information in a concise manner. Marzano gives us a summary of the generalizations of research on note-taking as follows.[169]

1. Verbatim note-taking is, perhaps, the least effective way to take notes. In the process of trying to record everything that is said or read, students fail to engage in the analysis and synthesis of the information.
2. Notes should be considered a work in progress – once the students have taken notes, they should be given time to add and revise their notes. This process if encouraged becomes a powerful activity for learning.
3. Notes should be used as study guides for tests – well written and sufficiently elaborated notes serve as great guides in preparation for exams.
4. The more notes that are taken the better – it is suggested that "less is more" is not a way to go with note-taking. Research seems to indicate a relationship between the number of notes taken and student achievement.

Homework and practice

Homework provides the students with an opportunity to deepen their understanding and skills in relation to the content they have learned beyond the confines of the classroom.

Marzano[170] gives us two purposes for giving homework to students. The first one is to help the students practice a concept they have learned well in

---
169. Marzano, Pickering, and Pollock, *Classroom Instruction*, 43–45.
170. Marzano, Pickering, and Pollock, 60–64.

class. It should be noted that practicing what has not been properly understood, will end up habituating errors or misconceptions. The second purpose for homework is for students to be prepared for the upcoming topic or elaborating on topics that have already been covered in class. Students may be required to do a prior reading on a topic before class. This would not require the learners to have a thorough understanding of it, but they would have read enough that they would be familiar with the material to be meaningfully engaged during class discussion. They can also be asked to elaborate on what has been covered in class.

Marzano also emphasizes the need to comment on homework. He quotes a study done by Walberg,[171] indicating that the effect of homework varied greatly depending on the feedback a teacher provided. Students who received written feedback had the highest performance.

Inquiry method

This is a form of discovery learning where the goal is for students to reason, derive general principles, and apply them to new situations. This method requires sufficient mastery of knowledge in the area for it to be a successful instructional strategy.[172] In this process students research into the nature of a problem with a view of finding some answers to why the problem exists. As students are searching, explaining, or interpreting unusual, unknown, or problematic phenomena, they gain a greater understanding of the subject matter. It develops the learners' ability for critical thinking and problem-solving.[173]

Reading quiz and examinations

This is a method for coercing students to read assigned readings and class notes. It is also a helpful tool for assessing students' comprehension. The kind of questions should encourage not a mindless regurgitation of the material but a higher level of learning.[174]

---

171. Walberg, "Productive Teaching," 75–104, quoted in Marzano, Pickering, and Pollock, *Classroom Instruction*, 64.
172. Schunk, *Learning Theories*, 268–69.
173. Mekonnen, *General Learning-Teaching Methods*, 153; Tomlinson, *Differentiated Classroom*, 91.
174. Mekonnen, *General Learning-Teaching Methods*, 277.

In-class presentation

Students who have worked on projects either in groups or as individuals are required to present their findings to the class. This falls under the individualized instructional methods because each individual has to organize their own thoughts on the section of the project they have worked on and creatively and clearly present to the class. Mekonnen suggests this to be extensively used in class considering its value for developing student communication skills and developing mastery of the concepts learned in class.[175]

Group Instructional Strategies

The group instructional methods are those where the learners are engaged in learning activities as a group. Some of the methods that will be covered under this category include discussion as a whole class and in small groups, group projects or assignments and field trips.

Discussion

Discussions can be whole-class discussions, or they can be small group discussions. Brookfield tells us that they can be used for intellectual, emotional, and sociopolitical purposes.[176]

It serves an intellectual purpose by providing students opportunities to explore the diversity of perspectives, increase students' awareness of and tolerance for ambiguity and complexity, and an opportunity to investigate their own assumptions. It also allows the students to develop the capacity for clear communication of ideas and skills of synthesis and integration.

As the students are involved in discussions, they will soon find out that they care about what others are saying about the topic, creating an emotional attachment to the topic being discussed. Discussions also give room for personal experiences to be shared and valued which brings dignity to individual experiences.

In a group, with a diversity of race, class, gender, learning style, etc., discussions also encourage attentive and respectful listening. It also helps the participants to learn the processes and habits of free discussion and the need to affirm others as key contributors to the discussions.

---

175. Mekonnen, 285.
176. Brookfield, *Skillful Teacher*, 119–24.

Whole-class discussion

Whole-class discussions provide opportunities for students to evaluate their own perceptions in light of the discussions in the classroom. However, in order for this to happen, there are a few things that need a teacher needs to recognize. Shaw gives us a number of qualities for facilitating a whole-class discussion, but only a few of them will be mentioned here. The first one is that the instructor should be able to spend a sufficient amount of time in setting reflective questions. Most of the time instructors tend to spend more time on the content rather than on the students' engagement in the learning process. Another helpful quality is the need to have a creative classroom setup, which is conducive for all students to speak and be clearly heard. A third quality, I would like to mention here is the need for quality non-verbal communication, which plays a very important role in fostering healthy class discussion. This can be created by moving away from the podium, keeping eye contact with the students to communicate value and relationship and also by giving time for students to reflect before speaking.[177]

As students are encouraged to evaluate their perceptions and are engaged in reflective thinking, questions will be raised in their minds. They would like clarifications and explanations of their dilemma. Therefore, it is also important that classroom discussion provides opportunities for students to ask questions. The teacher may not need to answer all the questions raised by the students but may allow other students to contribute to answering the question that was raised. At times, in a rush to finish the set content, students' questions go unanswered. Perry Shaw says, "less is more"[178] indicating that what is important is not necessarily that the instructor completes delivering the content but that the students are learning.

Small group discussion

Discussions can also be done in small groups of two-four students working together on a question or a task set by the teacher. Asking each of the groups to give responses to the task will give the students an incentive to do the work. While the instructor restrains from giving their perspective on the responses from each of the groups, they will give a brief answer to the

---

177. Shaw, *Transforming Theological Education*, 186–89; Davis, *Tools for Teaching*, 65.
178. Shaw, *Transforming Theological Education*, 185.

entire class when the groups are done in order to dispel any misinformation during the discussion.[179]

Group assignments

In this instructional strategy, students carry out project works in groups of two or more. Each group is given a task to cooperatively work on and present its findings to the larger group. Although it is designed to be a cooperative work, experience has shown that students take advantage of others and not be actively engaged in the project. This makes the methodology a hiding place for students who are not willing to put any effort into the work. It also makes it difficult to assess individual contributions to the project. In spite of this challenge of the method, it allows students to develop both cognitive and non-cognitive objectives at a high level. It also helps develop interpersonal skills as members of the group work through the project together.[180]

Field trips

These are planned and organized educational tours, visits, or journeys to a particular place. Trips are planned so as to facilitate the understanding of students regarding certain processes or concepts, that is as to how it works in real life as compared with the theoretical aspect taught in the classroom. Trips are made for students to see in practice what they studied. They are a useful instructional tool for providing a first-hand learning experience, making learning more meaningful and lasting, and giving an opportunity for improving social relationships among students and between students and the teachers.[181]

Interpersonal Relationships in Transformative Learning

The apostle Paul is one of those men who has influenced many through his teaching and life. A closer look at how he did it shows us that it is within a context of a relationship, a life lived among those he ministered to, as empowered by the Holy Spirit, that he was able to have an influence on many.

---

179. Davis, *Tools for Teaching*, 169; Schunk, *Learning Theories*, 271.
180. Mekonnen, *General Learning-Teaching Methods*, 245.
181. Nacino-Brown, Oke, and Brown, *Curriculum and Instruction*, quoted in Mekonnen, *General Learning-Teaching Methods*, 254.

He explains this in saying, "our gospel came to you not simply with words, but also with power, with the Holy Spirit and deep conviction. You know how we lived among you for your sake. You became imitators of us and the Lord" (1 Thess 1:5–6). A life-giving change is possible within the context of a relationship. Banks describes such life-giving relationships saying, "Truth must be embodied as well as articulated, incarnated as well as revealed. Doing this sometimes drains the life out of the one who is sharing with others but is precisely this that brings the greatest life to them."[182] He goes on to quote Parker J. Palmer who describes it so well by saying, "we do not just present truth, we must represent it to others. We do not just relate the truth in the hope that others might comprehend it, we relate to them in a way that helps them begin to be apprehended by it."[183]

Kathleen King, after a study of 137 college students who reported to have experienced a perspective transformation, made the following conclusion: in response to the contributing factors for perspective transformation 68.6 percent said learning activities, 41.6 percent said life change, and 70 percent said people. This study showed that the roles of people and learning activities were pronounced in the transformative learning of the students. This finding confirms the significant role of personal interaction and active participation in the transformative education experience.[184] Gerke, in his study of close to 600 participants at the evangelical faith-based adult non-formal education in midwestern United States also concluded that influential individuals significantly predicted or explained the perceived transformation.[185]

The quality of the relationship teachers have with students is key to the entirety of teaching.[186] In his study, Marzano found out that "if the relationship between the teacher and the students is good, then everything else seems to be enhanced."[187]

Merriam also agrees that relationships are an important part of transformative learning. She gives a couple of studies as an example of this. The first

---

182. Banks, *Reenvisioning Theological Education*, 172.
183. Banks, 174.
184. King, *Handbook of the Evolving Research*, Kindle Location, 1217–1219.
185. Gerke, "Learning Experiences," 100.
186. Marzano, *Art and Science of Teaching*, 149.
187. Marzano, 150.

example she gives is the study done by Harvie,[188] where he concludes that the transformative learning process for undergraduates had interpersonal support as an important component of the process. She also gives the example of the study done by Hwang who also concludes that the participants experienced transformative learning through relationship dialogue based on the relationships among group members and the relationship with God more than rational discourse.[189]

Marzano gives two components of an effective teacher-student relationship. The first one is dominance, which is related to the teacher's ability to demonstrate clarity of purpose and strong guidance. The purpose and guidance are demonstrated both academically and also in behavior. Academically, the teacher is able to provide guidance regarding academic content. In relation to behavioral guidance, the teacher is able to set and maintain clear classroom rules and procedures. Another aspect of dominance is the ability to develop emotional objectivity, which Marzano describes as being one who:

> Implements and enforces rules and procedures, execute disciplinary actions, and (even) cultivates effective relationships with students without interpreting violations of classroom rules and procedures, negative reactions to disciplinary actions, or lack of response to the teacher's attempts to forge relationships as a personal attack.[190]

Brophy and Everson described their observation saying, "We thought that the warmer, more affectionate teachers generally would be more effective than other teachers. As it turned out, teacher affectionateness did not show this relationship. It was unrelated, either linearly or curvilinearly, to students' learning gains."[191] Marzano concludes that teachers need to demonstrate emotional objectivity by not taking students' inappropriate classroom behavior

---

188. Harvie, "Transformative Learning," 3717A.

189. Hwang, "Relationships," quoted in Merriam, Caffarella, and Baumgartner, *Learning in Adulthood*, 153.

190. Marzano, Marzano, and Pickering, *Classroom Instruction*, quoted in Marzano, *Art and Science of Teaching*, 151.

191. J. E. Brophy and C. M. Evertson, *Learning from Teaching*, quoted in Marzano, *Art and Science of Teaching*, 152.

personally. This does not, however, mean that the teacher should avoid entering into a relationship with the students.[192]

The second component of an effective teacher-student relationship is cooperation, which involves demonstrating concern for each student and building a sense of community within the classroom. Teacher behavior is the language of relationships. "Students 'listen' to every behavior made by the teacher as a statement of the type of relationship the teacher desires, even when the teacher's actions have no such intent."[193] A report of teacher interactions with students by Harris and Rosenthal indicated that eye contact, gestures, smiles, encouragement, touch, praise, frequent interactions, and the duration of interactions have improved teacher-student relationships.[194] These behaviors imply that there is an emotional component to an effective teacher-student relationship. Positive emotions tend to develop a sense of concern and cooperation.[195]

Chapter Summary

As it is stated in the Lausanne Movement's Cape Town Commitment, the purpose of theological education is to strengthen and accompany the mission of the church.[196] This intent should govern the manner education happens within the theological higher educational institutions. Another major guiding principle in deciding how education should occur should be the recognition that man is created in the image of God and redeemed through the work of the Lord Jesus Christ. That recognition should make a difference in the manner education happens.

Over the years, many have developed theories of adult learning. Jack Mezirow has proposed a theory of perspective transformation that included ten stages of transformation. The two other key theories that were included in this study were the experiential learning by David Kolb and the transformative

---

192. Marzano, *Art and Science of Teaching*, 152.
193. Marzano, 152.
194. Harris and Rosenthal, "Mediation," 363–86, quoted in *Marzano, Art and Science of Teaching*, 152–53.
195. Marzano, *Art and Science of Teaching*, 153.
196. Lausanne Movement, "Cape Town Commitment," II.F.4.

learning cycle developed by Duane Elmer. A combination of these three was helpful in setting the theoretical framework for this research.

Although transformative learning is presented by Mezirow as being primarily a cognitive process, much of the research indicated that transformative learning included more than just the cognitive as previously stated. A truly transformative learning experience is one that is holistic which involves not only the cognition but also the affect and the behavior (skill).

CHAPTER 3

Methodological Design

Research Purpose

The purpose of this mixed method of study is to determine the factors that may predict or explain the students' self-reported transformation or the lack of it as a result of their study at the ACTEA-related theological institutions in Ethiopia. The determination of such factors within the Ethiopian context will help improve the quality of learning provided within the theological higher educational institutions and as a result, improve the quality of graduates that engage in strengthening the church as it carries out the mission of God.

Research Questions

The study seeks to answer the following research questions:

1. To what extent do students studying at the ACTEA-related theological colleges in Ethiopia understand themselves to have had a transformative learning experience?

2. To what extent do instructional strategies predict or explain self-reported transformative learning in students studying at the ACTEA-related theological colleges in Ethiopia?

    H_o1: There is no statistically significant relationship between the perceived transformative learning and the instructional strategies used in class and out of class within the ACTEA-related theological institutions in Ethiopia.

3. Is there is a difference between the teachers' and the students' perceptions of the instructional strategies that predict student transformative learning experience?

    H_o2: There is no statistically significant difference in the perceptions of the students and the teachers on the predictive relationship of the perceived transformative learning and the instructional strategies used in class and out of class within the ACTEA-related theological institutions.

4. To what extent do student interactions with other individuals in the college predict or explain self-reported transformative learning experience in students studying at the ACTEA-related theological colleges in Ethiopia?

    H_o3: There is no statistically significant relationship between the students' perceived transformative learning and their interactions with other individuals within the college.

5. To what extent is the self-reported transformative learning experience of students in full-time study different from those in part-time studies?

    H_o4: There is no statistically significant relationship between the students' perceived transformative learning and their program of study.

Research Methodology

This research is a cross-sectional survey of graduating students at five of the evangelical theological higher educational institutions in Ethiopia, which have some level of accreditation with ACTEA. In order to gain a more complete picture of the problem, a triangulation of different approaches to research is utilized in this study. Triangulation is defined as "the process of using multiple methods, data collection strategies, and data sources to obtain a more complete picture of what is being studied and to cross-check information."[1]

Therefore, a triangulation mixed methods design is used in this study where quantitative and qualitative data are equally

---

1. Gay, Mills, and Airasian, *Educational Research*, 405.

weighted and are collected concurrently throughout the same study – the data are not collected in separate studies or district phases. One method may be dominant over the other, or the two methods may be given equal weight throughout. When quantitative methods are dominant (QUAN-qual), for example, researchers might enliven their quantitative findings by collecting and writing case vignettes.[2]

In this approach, both quantitative and qualitative data are collected. The qualitative data was used to confirm the data collected through the quantitative method.[3]

The quantitative data is collected using a survey that provides a quantitative or numeric description of trends, attitudes, or opinions of a population by studying a sample of that population. Generalizations to the population will then be possible to be drawn from the sample results.[4] This design enables us to collect data from a relatively large sample, which would allow for better generalizability of the result to the population.

A transformative learning survey instrument was used to collect data from students in their last year of study at five different ACTEA related colleges in Ethiopia. The collection of this data helped to establish the relationship of students' classroom experiences and other college-related experiences to their perceived experience of transformative learning. The instructors also completed a similar survey in order to help explain the survey results of the students and make a comparison for any difference in the perception of the students and that of the instructors. The difference in the perception of the students and that of the instructors on the extent the learning activities predict or explain student transformative learning experience was done using the t-test statistic.

The analysis of variance (ANOVA) was used in comparing the perceived transformative learning experiences at the different theological institutions. A multiple and simple regression analysis was used to determine the extent the instructional strategies, interpersonal relationships, and mode of education predict or explain the perceived transformative learning experiences

---

2. Gay, Mills, and Airasian, 491.
3. Creswell, *Research Design*, 14.
4. Creswell, 12.

of the students. In doing the multiple regression the sequential blockwise regression analysis, which is also referred to as sequential multiple regression or hierarchical multiple regression, was used. This method allowed the researcher to examine the influence of several predictor independent variables (IV) in a specific order allowing for the determination of the variance each IV accounted for, above and beyond, what has been explained by any variable entered prior.[5]

Focus group discussions and classroom observations at each of the five institutions were the sources of the qualitative data. The participants in the focus groups were from among those who completed the survey. The deans of each of the colleges selected the participants using the random sampling method. This was important because it was believed that the more the two samples are similar the better the comparison.[6] In comparing the results, "the qualitative data collection is directly compared with results from quantitative data collection. Statistical trends are supported by qualitative themes or vice versa."[7] In this research, the qualitative themes have supported and helped better understand the quantitative findings.

Research Population and Sample

There are a number of Bible colleges that are run by different denominations across the country. The Ethiopian Ministry of Education does not provide accreditation to institutions that offer religious education in the country. Therefore, a number of the Bible colleges are run under the umbrella of the denominations and they do not have any kind of accreditation.

The Association for Christian Theological Education in Africa (ACTEA) is a ministry of the Association of Evangelicals of Africa (AEA), having been constituted as a project of its Theological and Christian Education Commission (TCEC) in 1976. ACTEA offers accreditation service and network and support services for evangelical theological education in Africa. In Ethiopia, the Ethiopian Graduate School of Theology is accredited at the

---

5. Aron, Arthur, and Coups, *Statistics for Psychology*, quoted in Mertler and Vannatta, *Advanced and Multivariate*, 170.

6. Creswell, *Research Design*, 148.

7. Gay, Mills, and Airasian, *Educational Research*, 493.

post-graduate level with ACTEA. The Mekane Yesus Seminary is accredited at both the undergraduate level as well as the post-graduate level. The Evangelical Theological College (ETC) is accredited at the undergraduate level. The Ethiopian Full Gospel Theological Seminary (EFGTS), Meserete Kristos College (MKC) and Shiloh Bible College Ethiopia (SBCE) have correspondent level accreditation. Pentecostal Theological College, Tabor Evangelical College, and Wolaita Evangelical Seminary have affiliate level relationship with ACTEA.[8]

The students at the post-graduate level have already gained a higher level of educational exposure and a number of them have completed their studies at the undergraduate level. Therefore, they were not included in this study. The colleges that were in an affiliate relationship with ACTEA were required to meet only three of the core academic standards (admissions, teaching staff qualifications, and length of program) in order to gain the affiliate status. These colleges had about four years to reach the level of candidacy and another four years to apply for full accreditation. Therefore, they were not included in the study. The colleges that were included in this study were those which were already fully accredited and those that had the candidacy status, which had started them on fulfilling all the standards for full accreditation. Therefore, this study was based on the three colleges that had gained the candidacy status (EFGTS, MKC, and SBCE) and the two that had full accreditation (ETC and MYS).

Limitation of Generalization

The theological colleges involved in this research are those that have undergraduate level programs. Therefore, although the conclusions of this research may be highly informative, it will not be completely transferable to theological colleges that offer diploma level or post-graduate-level training. The theological colleges involved in this research are primarily situated in the urban setting, which may make the generalization of its conclusions difficult to some of the colleges situated in the rural part of Ethiopia.

The factors that are considered in this study are limited to the classroom instructional strategies, interpersonal relationships, and whether the students

---

8. ACTEA, "Accredited Programmes and Institutions."

are studying on a part-time or full-time basis. Other possible factors that may contribute to the students' transformative learning experiences are not included.

The transformative learning framework used to measure the extent of the transformative learning experience was related to cognition, affect, and behavior. Other possible areas of transformation were not directly measured in this study.

The study is based on students' self-report of a perceived transformative learning experience. Because the instrument that is used is based on self-report, attitudes, interest, values, it suffers from some problems. It is not possible to be sure that the individuals expressed their true attitude, interest, values, or personality.[9]

Instrumentation

The instrument used in this research is a modification of the Learning Activities Survey (LAS) developed by Dr. Kathleen King. The LAS has been used by several researchers over many years with some modifications. It is designed to identify possible activities that contribute to learners' perspective transformation in relation to their educational experience. It makes use of the ten stages of transformative learning proposed by Jack Mezirow. Although some of the literature points out that it is not sufficiently tested for validity and reliability,[10] many have used it to measure transformative learning in different contexts.

Madsen used the LAS in her study on the transformative learning experiences students had at Abu Dhabi Women's College (ADWC). Gerke used the revised version of the instrument Madsen had developed in his study.[11] This researcher consulted both instruments in revising King's LAS and has developed one that was more fitting to the context where it was used and the proposed theoretical framework. Their instruments may be found in their articles.

---

9. Gay, Mills, and Airasian, *Educational Research*, 132.
10. Stuckey, Taylor, and Cranton, "Developing a Survey," 211–28.
11. Gerke, "Learning Experiences."

In the original LAS, respondents were required to check off or respond with a yes/no to a number of the questions. In its first section, it provides thirteen items that are designed to measure Mezirow's ten stages of perspective transformation. An item or two were set to measure each of these stages. The participants completing the instrument were to check off the statement that would apply to them. The instrument measured three levels of perspective transformation namely PT-Index = 3, for having perspective transformation in relation to education; PT-Index = 2, for perspective transformation not associated to education; and PT-Index = 1, for lack of perspective transformation.[12]

Madsen uses a five-point Likert scale of agreement or influence in her revised instrument. She revised the first section of the instrument that was designed to determine transformative learning experience and came up with eighteen items that were set on a five-point Likert scale. The eighteen items were designed to measure three constructs namely: perception of change in self and others (a = .59), considering and making changes in thought and action (a = .81), and awareness of the benefit of change and prediction of future behavior (a = .86).

In this study, King's instrument was used with some elements added to it from Madsen's revised instrument as described in the instrument description below. Madsen's instrument was helpful in structuring the instrument and setting the items on a Likert scale instead of the yes/no format used by King. Although the constructs identified by the researcher were different and based on a different theoretical framework, the idea of having constructs for transformative learning came from Madsen's study. Since Gerke's study was set in a different context, the instrument was not used in this study.[13]

Instrument Description

The instrument used in this study has four sections. The first section sought to determine the degree of transformative learning the learner experienced while studying at the college. There are three questions included in the instrument to determine the students' perceived transformative learning. Question 1 uses

---

12. King, *Handbook of Evolving Research*, Kindle Locations 578–580.

13. Permission was received from Dr. Kathleen King to use the instrument in this research, and from Dr. Susan Madsen to use her instrument as needed.

nineteen items to determine degrees of transformative learning, question 2 requires students to respond with a yes/no to the presence of transformative learning and question 3 asks the students to give examples that give evidence to the perceived transformative learning if any.

The second section measured the extent the students' perceived transformative learning was influenced by their interpersonal relationships. In order to do this, questions 4, 5, and 6 were used. Question 4 had seven items listing possible influences set on a four-point Likert scale of strongly agree to strongly disagree. Question 5 asked the students to respond with a yes/no to the presence of an interpersonal relationship. Question 6 asked the participants to give examples of the different influences they experienced while studying at the college.

The third section dealt with the instructional strategies that may have contributed to the students' perceived transformative learning experiences. The two questions in this section (question 7 and question 8) measured the frequency the instructional strategies were used and the influence each of the instructional strategies had on the students' perceived transformative learning experiences.

The last section of the instrument provided the demographics of the participants and it helped in understanding the background of the participants and the exploration of a possible difference of transformative learning across different demographic data.

Validity and Reliability

The original (LAS) had an internal consistency reliability coefficient of .858.[14] Madsen's revised instrument had a reliability of .59 for the perception of change, .81 for considering making change, and .86 for awareness and prediction.[15] Since the instrument used in this study was significantly modified from both the LAS and Madsen's revised version of it, it was necessary to establish reliability and validity of the instrument. In order to help with its content validity, the researcher shared the instrument with a group of experts who provided their feedback to the survey instrument. The experts who gave feedback on the survey instrument included:

---

14. King, Kindle Location 2805.
15. Madsen and Cook, "Transformative Learning," 13.

- Dr. Robert Ferris – Professor Emeritus, Columbia Biblical Seminary and School of Missions, Columbia International University; PhD from Michigan State University.
- Dr. John Jusu – Overseas Council International, Africa coordinator and professor at Africa International University; PhD from Trinity International University.
- Dr. Frew Tamrat – Principal and Professor at Evangelical Theological College, Addis Ababa, Ethiopia; PhD in Educational Studies from Columbia International University
- Dr. Philip Walker – President of International Christian Ministries, PhD in Adult Education and Organizational Development from Walden University Minneapolis.
- Dr. Perry Shaw – Adjunct Professor of Education at Arab Baptist Theological Seminary, Lebanon; EdD from Asia Graduate School of Theology.
- Dr. Seblewengel Asrat – Professor of Education at the Evangelical Theological College, Addis Ababa, Ethiopia; PhD in Educational Studies from Trinity International University.

The suggestions from the experts were included in the instrument and the procedure used for pilot testing.

In order to test for reliability of the instrument, a pilot test with twelve of the ETC graduating students was done. The data from the pilot test was coded and analyzed using the Statistical Package for Social Sciences (SPSS). The Cronbach's alpha for all the items related to transformative learning, interpersonal relationship, and instructional strategies was .904, which indicated high reliability. A discussion with all the twelve participants in the pilot test led to the inclusion of an additional item to the measurement on interpersonal relationships. It also helped the researcher see that the students were most comfortable with the Amharic version of the instrument rather than the English. Therefore, although both the Amharic and English versions of the instrument were made available for all participants, except for the foreign students, most of the students completed the survey in Amharic.

Exploratory Factor Analysis – Transformative Learning Experience

A principal component factor analysis (PCA) using varimax (VAR) with the Kaiser normalization rotation method was done on each of the three major scales namely, transformative learning (question 1), interpersonal relationship (question 4), and instructional strategies (questions 7 and 8). The results of each factor analysis are briefly discussed below.

The first section of the instrument had a question that had nineteen items, measured on a four-point Likert scale of strongly agree to strongly disagree, and was used to measure perceived transformation of the students. The Cronbach's alpha for the nineteen items was .92 indicating strong reliability of the scale.

The nineteen items were grouped into three subscales, which measured the degree of perceived transformative learning: (1) Awareness of the need for transformation, (2) reflective practice, and (3) integrative generation. Items 1.1–1.6 are related to awareness of the need for transformation. Items 1.7–1.12 are related to reflective practice. Finally, the remaining items, 1.13–1.19 are related to the integrative generation. Each of the subscales had at least two items that measured cognition, affect, and psychomotor. The nineteen items were subject to principal component factor analysis using varimax with Kaiser normalization rotation method. This resulted in four factors with eigenvalues greater than one excluding one item (see table 1).

Table 1. Loadings of Perception of Transformative Learning Experience

No	Items	Need to Change $\alpha = .737$	Willing to Change $\alpha = .686$	Reflective Practice $\alpha = .807$	Integrative Generation $\alpha = .857$
1.1	Learned new things I did not know before	**.831**	.133	.277	.021
1.2	Able to explain concepts I did not know before	**.757**	.082	.074	.433
1.3	Open to listen to new ideas	.080	**.737**	-.007	.227
1.4	Open to engage in conversations I did not agree with	.455	**.600**	.095	.191

No	Items	Need to Change α = .737	Willing to Change α = .686	Reflective Practice α = .807	Integrative Generation α = .857
1.5	There were times when I developed a desire to act and do things differently	.196	-.075	**.815**	.209
1.6	There were occasions when I decided to change or revise some of my beliefs or the way I did somethings	.169	.063	**.702**	.365
1.7	I have considered ways I may start to act differently from my usual beliefs and way of doing things	.202	.358	**.575**	.107
1.8	I have tried to figure out how I may adopt these new ways of acting to my life and ministry	.070	.354	**.551**	.274
1.9	I gathered the information I needed to adopt these new ways of acting	.272	.199	.147	**.632**
1.10	I tried to practice some of the new things I learned so that I would become more comfortable or confident in doing them	.243	**.400**	.342	.356
1.11	I started to act and do somethings differently from the way I used to	.003	**.675**	.373	.129
1.12	I have grown in my ability to solve problems in my personal life and ministry	.124	.274	.209	**.569**
1.13	I am better equipped to judge the values of certain ideas and practices	.072	.097	.228	**.715**

No	Items	Need to Change α = .737	Willing to Change α = .686	Reflective Practice α = .807	Integrative Generation α = .857
1.14	My studies at the college have changed some of my points of view on certain issues and practices	-.008	.292	.407	**.580**
1.15	I now behave differently in some ways because of the change I had in my point of views	.037	.321	**.531**	.439
1.17	Because I have started doing somethings differently, I see a change in my life and ministry	.017	.339	.493	**.572**
1.18	I was able to generate ideas that enabled me to do things better	.177	.193	.237	**.689**
1.19	There are somethings I have learned to do without hesitation	.105	.047	.128	**.725**

Note: Factor loadings ≥ .40 are in boldface. Item 16 was the same as item 11, so it was removed.

The items in the first subscale (awareness of change) were split into two scales namely awareness of the need to change and willingness to change. Therefore, four factors were identified for this study – (1) awareness of the need to change, (2) willingness to change, (3) reflective practice, and (4) integrative generation.

A correlation of the four subscales produced a strong correlation between the three subscales (reflective practice, integrative generation, and willingness to change) and a moderate correlation between awareness of the need to change and the other subscales (see table 2).

Table 2. Subscale Inter-Correlations

	Awareness of Need to Change	Willingness to Change	Reflective Practice	Integrative Generation
Awareness of need to change	1	.433**	.441**	.455**
Willingness to change	.433**	1	.618**	.643**
Reflective practice	.441**	.618**	1	.721**
Integrative generation	.455**	.643**	.721**	1

** Correlation is significant at the 0.01 level (2-tailed). N = 137, p < .001

The principal component factor analysis using varimax with Kaiser normalization rotation fixed at seven factors aligned the items very closely to what was originally planned (three factors in figure 10). However, for the sake of minimizing the factors, the four components identified with eigenvalues above one was used in this study.

Exploratory Factor Analysis – Interpersonal Relationship

The second section of the instrument sought to determine the different interpersonal and other non-educational experiences the students may have had while studying at the college, which they perceive to have contributed to their transformative learning experience. The interpersonal influences in question 4 included the influences of the instructors, academic staff, and other students.

A factor analysis of the influence of the interpersonal relationship scale comprised of seven items was done using the principal component analysis extraction method and a varimax Kaiser normalization rotation. It confirmed two factors namely teachers and administrative staff that had five of the items, and students that had two of the items as shown in table 3.

Table 3. Factor Loadings of Interpersonal Relationships

No	Items	Teachers and Admin $\alpha = .838$	Other Students $\alpha = .832$
1.1	Teachers' in-class influence	**.833**	.172
1.2	Teachers' out-of-class influence	**.859**	.155
1.3	Teachers' influence in their effort to teach	**.816**	.250
1.4	Teachers' modeling influence	**.744**	.337
1.5	Students' in-class influence	.248	**.885**
1.6	Students' out-of-class influence	.238	**.885**
1.7	Influence of admin staff	**.621**	.379

Note: Factor loadings are in boldface.

Pearson's correlation indicated a moderate correlation between the teachers and admin subscale and the students' subscale (r = .545, p = 0.00, N = 137). Therefore, two scales were set to measure the interpersonal relationships: (1) Teachers and administrative staff and (2) the students.

Exploratory Factor Analysis – Instructional Strategies

The third section of the instrument dealt with identifying the possible instructional strategies that may have contributed to the learners' transformative learning experience or the lack of it. The questions related to this are questions 7 and 8. Question 7 has nineteen items set on a five-point frequency continuous Likert scale (very frequently, frequently, sometimes, rarely, and never). Question 8 had the same nineteen instructional strategies. It was formulated to determine the influence of each of the instructional strategies on the students' perceived transformative learning experience. The items in this question were set on a four-point Likert scale of influence (very influential, influential, slightly influential, and not influential at all).

Factor analysis of the frequency of the different instructional strategies (question 7) (n=120; α = .888) and the influence of each of the instructional strategies on the perceived transformative learning experience (question 8) (n=120; α = .891) resulted in no specific factors. Although based on the literature review, it was hoped to have three scales (mass instructional methods, group learning methods, and individualized methods), the factor analysis was not able to identify underlining relationships among the different instructional strategies to yield specific useful factors. Therefore, the instructional strategies comprised of the nineteen items formed one scale.

Variable, research question, and item correlation. The relationship between the different items to the research questions and the variables is shown in figure 12.

Variable	Research Question	Questionnaire Items
Instructional Strategies	RQ2. To what extent do instructional strategies used in class predict or explain self-reported transformative learning in students studying at the ACTEA related theological colleges in Ethiopia?	See question 7 and question 8. Classroom activities contributing to transformative learning and the frequency of their use.
Inter-personal relationship	RQ4. To what extent do student interactions with other individuals in the college predict or explain self-reported transformative learning experience in students studying at the ACTEA-related theological colleges in Ethiopia?	See questions 4, 5, and 6. Influence of teachers, other administration and support staff and other students.
Type of Program	RQ5. To what extent is the self-reported transformative learning experience of students in full-time study different from those in part-time studies?	See question 10. Students in either the full-time program or part-time study.
Demographic Information		See questions 9, 11, 12, and 13

Figure 12: Variable, research question, and item correlation chart

Research Process and Data Collection

The purpose of this research was to determine the extent undergraduate students who were in their graduating year perceived to have experienced transformative learning. In addition, the researcher sought to determine any predictive factors that may have contributed towards the students' perceived transformative learning or the lack of it. In order to make these determinations, a mixed method of both descriptive and inferential statistics was used.

The participants in this research were from five theological colleges that have undergraduate programs. The researcher contacted the heads of each college in order to receive permission to carry out the research. Upon receiving permission, the researcher was introduced to the academic deans of each of the institutions to identify the students in their graduating year and carry out the research. The academic deans and in one case the dean of students were able to identify two or three graduating students to serve as an assistant to the researcher. Each part of the survey was explained to them as they completed it. Once that was done, the assistant students at each of the institutions divided among themselves the graduating students, and they individually contacted each of the graduating students and brought in the completed survey. The assistants were compensated for the work they did. The students who completed the surveys also received an incentive through the academic deans in appreciation for taking their time in completing it. This process helped the researcher in getting a good response rate of 92 percent, and it is believed that since many of them completed the survey with the assistants, the response is relatively more reliable. The reliability of the data was increased because it was less likely that students would have marked their answers without reading the questions while they completed the survey with research assistants.

In order to help with triangulation, a focus group discussion with students who were randomly selected from among those who turned in their completed surveys was conducted. A set of seven open-ended questions were used to guide the discussion. A voice recorder was used to record the discussion. Since the discussion was done in the national language of the country (Amharic), it was necessary not only to transcribe but also translate into English. The researcher, who is proficient in both languages, completed the transcription and translation of all five focus group discussions. In order to ensure correct transcription and translation of the discussions, two professors, who were proficient in both languages, were requested to listen to five minutes of each of the focus group discussions and compare to the translation. Both professors confirmed that the translations correctly captured the ideas discussed in the focus group (see appendix H).

The perspective of the teachers was also gained using the survey instrument that had similar questions to the one used with the students. The questions in the survey for the teachers had one item that sought to determine the teachers' perception of students' transformative experience. A second question asked the teachers to indicate the extent they perceive that students' inter-personal relationships contributed to their transformative learning experience. A couple of items (questions 4 and 5) were included in the survey to determine the frequency teachers use the different instructional strategies and the extent they perceive them to have influenced the students' transformative learning experience.

The conclusions of this study were strengthened by the multiple ways data was gathered. Besides the survey and the focus group discussions, the researcher observed nine class sessions at the five colleges. Two classes were observed at each of the four colleges and one class at the fifth college. Each of the observed classes had different students and instructors. The academic deans at each of the institutions selected the classes to be observed depending on the classes that were offered on the days the researcher visited the campus. The academic deans informed the instructors ahead of time of the researcher's visit to their class, so they were not caught by surprise.

In each of the colleges, the researcher took notes on the different instructional strategies that were used and the extent the students interacted with the teacher, each other, and the subject matter. The various instructional strategies used at each of the institutions were thematically grouped into categories. A descriptive analysis of each of these categories provided helpful information in triangulating the quantitative data gathered on the instructional strategies that were used.

The results of the findings from the survey, the focus group discussions, and the classroom observations are discussed in the next chapter.

CHAPTER 4

Analysis of Findings

Introduction

This research is a cross-sectional survey of graduating students at five of the evangelical theological higher educational institutions in Ethiopia, which have some level of accreditation with ACTEA. The study used a probability sampling where all graduating students at the five colleges had an equal probability of being selected to participate in the study.[1]

The purpose of this research was to determine the degree the graduating students from these institutions perceived to have had a transformative learning experience as a result of their study at the colleges. It also sought to explore the extent to which interpersonal relationships, instructional strategies, and the time spent in the program, predict or explain the perceived transformative learning experiences students had.

In order to do this, triangulation mixed methods design is used in this study where, "quantitative and qualitative data are equally weighted and are collected concurrently throughout the same study."[2] This chapter presents data collected to answer the five research questions of this study. Since the purpose of this study is not to make a comparison between the different institutions, the researcher intends to maintain the anonymity of the results and not make a connection between the results and any of the institutions.

---

1. Gay, Mills, and Airasian, *Educational Research*, 112.
2. Gay, Mills, and Airasian, 491.

Therefore C1, C2, C3, C4, and C5 are randomly used to refer to the different institutions in presenting the results.

The discussion of each of the research questions includes analysis of (a) quantitative data obtained through the survey instrument distributed to the students; (b) quantitative data obtained from teachers' perception of the frequency and degree of influence of the instructional strategies they used; (c) focus group discussion at each of the five institutions; and (d) classroom observation at each of the institutions.

There were 137 responses out of the 149 surveys distributed to students from all the five institutions. The response breakdown of the response rate is given in table 4.

Table 4. Student Survey Response Rate

Institution	No. Distributed	No. Responding	%
C1	44	41	93
C2	17	16	94
C3	34	32	94
C4	28	24	85
C5	26	24	92
Total	149	137	92

There were thirty-one teacher responses out of thirty-four surveys distributed to teachers at the five institutions. The breakdown of the responses of the teachers from the different institutions is given in table 5. The teachers who were given the survey were those who taught at least two courses at the institution they are associated with.

Table 5. Teacher Survey Response Rates

Institution	No. Distributed	No. of Responses	%
C1	11	11	100
C2	6	5	83
C3	6	6	100
C4	6	5	83
C5	5	4	83
Total	34	31	91

Purposive sampling was used in the selection of students who would be a part of the focus group discussion. Students who completed the survey and were willing to join the focus group were invited to participate. The number of focus group participants at each of the institutions is displayed in table 6.

Table 6. Focus Group Participants

Institution	No. of Participants
C1	8
C2	16
C3	6
C4	6
C5	6
Total	42

Classroom observations were done at all five institutions. Of these, two classes were observed at each of the four colleges and one class was observed at one of the colleges, since there was no second class available for observation during the period the research was carried out.

Presentation and Analysis of the Data

Research Question 1

To what extent do students studying at the ACTEA related theological colleges in Ethiopia understand themselves to have had a transformative learning experience?

Students' Perception of Transformative Learning.

The exploratory factor analysis for the nineteen items in question 1 identified the items that "go together"[3] as shown in table 7. The table also provides a descriptive and frequency analysis for each of the items in question 1. Item 1, which measures knowledge of new things and belongs to the "Awareness of need to change" construct, has the highest mean. Item 19, which measures the development of a new habit where one is able to do something without any hesitation, has the lowest mean. This item belongs to the "integrative generation" construct.

Table 7. Student's Perception of Transformative Learning Experience

Scale		Items	n	M	SD	% Agreement
Aware of the need to change	1.1	Learned new things I did not know before	137	3.81	0.41	99.30
	1.2	Able to explain concepts I did not know before	136	3.70	0.48	99.30

---

3. Polit and Hungler, *Nursing Research*.

Scale		Items	n	M	SD	% Agreement
Willingness to change	1.3	Open to listen to new ideas	136	3.69	0.48	99.30
	1.4	Open to engage in conversations I did not agree with	137	3.64	0.50	94.20
	1.10	I tried to practice some of the new things I learned so that I would become more comfortable or confident in doing them	136	3.61	0.52	98.50
	1.11	I started to act and do somethings differently from the way I used to	137	3.45	0.64	93.40
Reflective practice	1.5	There were times when I developed a desire to act and do things differently	136	3.56	0.57	96.30
	1.6	There were occasions when I decided to change or revise some of my beliefs or the way I did somethings	137	3.58	0.60	94.20
	1.7	I have considered ways I may start to act differently from my usual beliefs and way of doing things	137	3.55	0.61	95.60
	1.8	I have tried to figure out how I may adopt these new ways of acting to my life and ministry	137	3.71	0.47	99.30
	1.15	I now behave differently in some ways because of the change I had in my point of views	136	3.44	0.61	95.60

Scale		Items	n	M	SD	% Agreement
Integrative generation	1.9	I gathered the information I needed to adopt these new ways of acting	137	3.65	0.49	99.30
	1.12	I have grown in my ability to solve problems in my personal life and ministry	137	3.61	0.56	97.80
	1.13	I am better equipped to judge the values of certain ideas and practices	137	3.58	0.58	97.10
	1.14	My studies at the college have changed some of my points of view on certain issues and practices.	137	3.63	0.58	96.40
	1.17	Because I have started doing some things differently, I see a change in my life and ministry	137	3.51	0.67	93.40
	1.18	I was able to generate ideas that enabled me to do things better	136	3.65	0.51	98.60
	1.19	There are some things I have learned to do without hesitation	136	3.40	0.68	91.90

Note: N=137; Item responses were on a four-point Likert scale (4 – strongly agree, 3 – agree, 2 – disagree, and 1 – strongly disagree). Percent agreement includes both agree and strongly agree. The remaining percentage that is not shown on the table is "disagree" and "strongly disagree."

A frequency and descriptive analysis of each of the four sub-scales, as given in table 8, shows that the mean score for all the subscales appears to be similar. It appears that most of the participants are reporting a high level of transformative learning. This finding is clarified later through the process of triangulation using the data gathered from the focus group discussion. However, a clear distinction can still be observed between the awareness of the need to change (M=3.76) and integrative generation (M=3.58). This is probably as one would expect to see in an educational institution where a higher number of students are likely to report transformation in relation to knowledge and understanding. A large number of students reported recognition of a need to change and a relatively lower number of the students reported having experienced a stage of the integrative generation where they have gone past the recognition of the need to change and have actually experienced change and were able to exhibit it automatically.

Table 8. Mean and Percentage of Subscales with Mean Greater Than Three

Response	M	SD	%
Awareness of the need to change	3.76	.398	99.3
Willingness to change	3.60	.386	95.6
Reflective practice	3.57	.430	94.2
Integrative generation	3.57	.426	92.7

Note: N=137, percent is for mean values greater than 3.

A one-way ANOVA was carried out to see if there is a difference in the students' perceived transformative learning experience among the students in the five institutions. The result showed that the difference among the institutions was not statistically significant for the transformative learning scale $F(4,132) = 1.464$, $p = .217$. The F-test also showed that there is no statistically significant difference among the institutions in relation to each of the four subscales: awareness of need – $F(4,132) = 1.793$, $p = .134$; willingness to change – $F(4,132) = .1.579$, $p = .184$; reflective practice – $F(4,132) = 1.342$, $p = .258$ and integrative generation – $F(4,132) = 1.538$, $p = .195$).

An item (question 2) was included in the instrument to indicate the participant's belief of change as a result of their study. The question stated "do you believe you have experienced a time when you realized that some of your values, beliefs, opinions or way you do things have changed as a result of your studies at the college?" For a sample of n=128, 92.2 percent of the students responded affirmatively while 7.8 percent replied negatively. In table 7, it was reported that 99.3 percent of the students have reported gaining new knowledge for n=137. The 7.8 percent of the respondents who responded negatively to question 2 may, therefore, be thinking of a level of transformation beyond gaining knowledge.

The quantitative data shows that over 90 percent of the students have reported that they had some level of a transformative learning experience. Examples of the changes they reported help in understanding their perceived transformative learning experiences. These examples will be presented in the following section.

Areas of Perceived Transformation

As a follow-up to the students' assertion of transformation, in question 3 participants were asked to give examples of change they have experienced. The question asked the participants to briefly describe some of the changes that happened as a result of their studies at the college. It was only ninety participants (65.7 percent) who responded to this question. The absence of response in question 3 may not lead to the conclusion of a lack of transformation since it is already clear from question 2 that 118 participants have already responded affirmatively to the presence of transformative learning. The students may have been more inclined to checking off a box rather than take time to write their responses.

The responses of the ninety participants are thematically organized to yield nine specific categories as shown in table 9.

Table 9. Areas of Perceived Transformation

Response	Frequency	%
Valuing spiritual practice	19	21.10
Valuing others	10	11.10
Character formation	28	31.10
Knowledge and understanding	44	48.90
Analysis and evaluation	13	14.40
Application and synthesis	32	35.60
Improved ministry skills	42	46.70
Imparting ministry skills	8	8.90
Improved social skills	15	16.70

Note: n=90

The nine categories in table 9 were broadly grouped to yield three categories based on similarities (table 10).

Table 10. Broad Categories of Perceived Areas of Change

Response	Frequency	%
Deep change (characterization)	57	63.30
Changed cognitive frame of reference	89	98.90
Skill formation	65	72.20

Note: n=90; areas mentioned are not exclusive of the other areas. The same students mentioned different areas.

A greater number of students have indicated transformation in the area of cognition. The perceived areas of transformation in characterization and skill are relatively lower. The participants from all institutions indicate a greater transformation in areas of cognition and different levels of transformation in relation to character and skill, as can be seen in table 11.

Table 11. Areas of Transformation Frequency by Institution

Response	C1 n=38		C2 n=8		C3 n=16		C4 n=16		C5 n=12	
	FQ	%	FQ	%	FQ	%	FQ	%	FQ	%
Deep change (characterization)	26	68	6	75	6	38	6	38	6	50
Changed cognitive frame of reference	31	82	7	88	13	81	14	88	12	100
Skill formation	24	63	2	25	12	75	13	81	10	83

Note: FQ – Frequency

In table 11, a much lower number of students reported a change in the area of skill formation in C2. As it will be discussed later in the discussion of the focus group, C2 participants indicated that they did not have much in relation to reported ministry or internships where the students are required to engage in ministry while studying at the college. It is possible that the low response in the skill formation may be due to the lack of Institutionally directed ministry engagement.

Focus Group Findings on Perceived Transformative Learning

This section presents the findings from all the five focus groups in response to seven questions. The answers to these questions provide clarity and depth to the questions asked through the survey instrument. The responses are reported question by question.

In responding to the question of whether students at the colleges experience change as a result of their studies at the college, all the participants from all the five colleges agreed that most of the students experienced some degree of transformation. One of the participants from C1 explained that it is impossible not to experience change after being at the college for four years. A number of the participants gave examples of change they experienced because of their studies at their respective colleges, which will be presented later in this section.

One participant from C4 agreed that students come seeking to experience change and that they do experience change in relation to their knowledge, which included the knowledge of the Bible. They went on to comment by saying, "However, we do not see much change in the life of the students. I find it difficult to say that the students fully achieve change in their lives." An observation by a C3 participant reinforced the same idea by saying,

> I do not think there will be an ethical change. But our ability to understand the Bible and the way we interpret the Bible will change in comparison to what we knew before. Because we are learning different sections of the Bible, our understanding of the Bible changes. But I am not sure there will be a change in character. It is not knowledge that brings change but, living it out is what brings character change.

Another participant from C3 agreed that close to 95 percent of the students experienced change while studying at the college. However, about 5 percent of them fail to have a transformative learning experience. They said that depending on "the way they come into the college – the motive they come with, the spirit they come with, they may come and not experience change."

There was no doubt among all the groups that there was a change in terms of their knowledge. The area that was in doubt related to the change in character and skill. One of the participants from C4 said,

> It will be difficult to say that whoever has come to know will also implement it in life. Sometimes a person may be passive. What they have come to know will remain dormant. As I said earlier, in my life, it has opened up opportunities to apply what I have come to know. I believe there is a change in my ministry. I have changed in my teaching and preaching. I am also able to explain things I used to struggle in explaining in the past.

A statement by a participant from C1 summarizes the ideas well: "for a person who joins C1 with purpose, there will be a big change." This hesitation to confirm transformation in the area of character and skill is also in line with the quantitative data found in tables 6 and 7, where the frequency of examples of change related to character and skill were relatively lower than the number of examples mentioned in the cognitive area.

As a follow-up to the discussion of the presence of a change in the lives of the students, the participants were asked to give examples of areas where they may have experienced change. The examples they mentioned fall into the following six categories.

Cognitive Skills. In relation to the cognitive skills, the participants mentioned changes related to knowledge, understanding, critical thinking, ability to see things differently, asking questions on how they served, and becoming more willing to change. A student at C1 said, "I no longer just see one thing. I ask questions. I see that in other students as well. They are very critical thinkers."

Perspective and Attitude Change. Some of the examples mentioned in this area included the ability to develop a biblical perspective on belief and practice and correct unbiblical understandings, expand views and perspectives, change what was traditionally held as being true, broaden the vision for ministry and life, and develop a correct attitude and approach towards the Bible. In expressing the change of attitude, a student at C1 said, "my attitude towards the word has changed in areas related to my heart, hand, and head." Another participant from the same college said, "the study has given me the reverence for the word. I used to give people what the Bible was not saying. Now, I have reverence for the eord, which is making me be careful to study and prepare well."

Skills Gained. The skills that were developed, included the ability to study effectively in the college, develop writing skills, skills in the studying and interpretation of the Bible, and skills related to preaching and teaching. A participant from C5 explains the skill they have gained in the way they studied and interpreted the Bible by saying, "We are able to clearly understand this [how to read and interpret the Bible] and be able to communicate the message of the Bible to the contemporary generation."

Changes in Character. The idea of change in character was mentioned several times but not very specifically. One student from C1 said, "Students do not just do things as they used to. There is a schedule for listening to the news, for studying, praying, and worship. It has made me become programmed."

Another student from C5 said, "I have personally seen a change in my life. Things I have removed from my own personal life – this would be in my behavior, the stand I take in life, and in decisions I now make."

Changes in Ministry Quality. There were a number of examples that were mentioned in relation to the changes in the quality of their ministry. They mentioned an improved ability to grow the church through evangelism and small groups, improved preparation to preach, teach, ability to explain things better, defend belief, and their ability to provide better management and administration to the ministries of the church and other organizations. One of the participants from C3 said, "the teachings equip the ministers. When the person leaves, they also leave with the capacity to be influential in the church with the quality of ministry they give. It helps them to give appropriate service."

Changes in Social Skills. A good number of the students have said that they have grown in their ability to relate with others. They mentioned being more patient and able to interact with people from diverse cultural backgrounds. In speaking of the development of ethical behavior or character, a student from C2 said,

> Ethical changes do not come only from the things we learn. What we are, are not all fully related to the things we learn in class. There are courses we learn about Bible interpretation and ethics, but the ethical changes come from living together in the community. It comes with friendship.

Contributors to Transformative Learning Experience

The participants of each of the focus groups were asked to list the possible contributors to the perceived transformative learning experiences students had. These contributors mentioned by all the groups were put into six categories. A summarized description of the factors found in each of the categories is given as follows.

Content related. This included exposure to the clear teaching of the word, exposure to different points of view, and course content that is learned. A participant from C1 said, "a clear, sound, and hermeneutically right presentation of the word has an influence on the students."

Teacher related. The teachers are mentioned as having a strong contribution to the perceived transformative learning experiences of the students. They are able to do this through their personality, their exemplary life in class and out of class, their approach to students, the effort they put in their teaching, their knowledge of the subject matter, their ability to motivate students, and the love they have for their students. All participants mentioned the personality and exemplary life of the teachers, as important contributors to the change students experience. On the other hand, one of the participants from C1 mentioned that as much as the personality of the teacher has the ability to positively influence students, they also have the ability to negatively affect the students when they display inappropriate behavior. They said, "there are some who are discouraged very much by the personality of the teachers."

The relationship the teachers have among themselves is also mentioned as being influential to the students who observe the way teachers relate with each other.

Student community related. The students believe that their experiences with other students have been strong contributors to their perceived transformative learning experience. Some of the factors related to students that contributed to their transformation included the time they spent in reading and studying together with other students, outside of class discussions, in-class group discussions, exemplary lives of other students, the care students showed towards each other when in need, times of fellowship and prayer, and living together with others who come from diverse cultural backgrounds.

College related. Some of the college-related factors are also mentioned as being contributors to the change that students experience. Some of these include the prayer and worship times organized by the colleges. In the case of C5, times of prayer and worship before class was mentioned as a strong contributor. Another one has to do with the system of accountability the college has set to encourage teachers to deliver their best in their work. It also holds students accountable to be present in class and abide by the policy the college has set for plagiarism and a high standard of behavior. The third area has to do with the facility the college provides, which includes the availability of library and internet facility and an environment conducive for teaching and learning. Finally, the curriculum design was also mentioned as a contributor. A student from C1 said that the clear workload for each of the courses encourages students to work hard and produce quality work.

Teaching process related. The methodologies the teachers use in their teaching, the notes they provide for the students and the different assignments such as reflections and presentations are mentioned as contributors to their perceived change.

Personal effort. Finally, they brought in the importance of the student putting an effort into their own learning. A student from C3 said, "I do not think that those who come without aim or purpose would experience change. So, the person who comes with purpose leaves changed." Students who come from a ministerial background are likely to come with a purpose. The fact that the students are able to spend time reflecting on what they are learning and time they commit to prayer and personal devotion are also contributors to the change they experience. A participant from C5 said that the "time a student gives for prayer and worship by themselves, with friends at the dorm, reading together with other students and studying together contributes to the student's transformation." Finally, as much as the teachers prepare and invest in the learning of the students, there is "also a need of submissiveness from the student" (C1) to work with diligence. Another participant from C1 explained the role of the student as follows:

> As students are more and more committed, they become more transformed. When they begin to do what they have learned, when they begin to treat God's word as the word of God, integrate the cognitive learning with their heart, are committed to the teaching method, and apply the things they are learning to their life with the help of the Holy Spirit, a person will experience transformation. So, there is the part of the student.

While this study is exploring interpersonal relationships and instructional strategies as the primary areas to explain the perception of students' transformative learning experience, the participants in the focus group have identified a few more possible factors. These included the students' effort in their own learning, aspects of the educational institution and the curriculum.

The findings on the extent of the interpersonal relationship and the instructional strategies contribute towards the students' perceived transformative learning experiences will be further discussed under the discussion of research questions 2, 4, and 5.

Research Question 2

To what extent do instructional strategies used in class and out of class predict or explain self-reported transformative learning in students studying at the ACTEA-related theological colleges in Ethiopia?

Null Hypothesis 1

There is no statistically significant relationship between the perceived transformative learning and the instructional strategies used within the ACTEA-related theological institutions in Ethiopia.

In order to determine the extent instructional strategies explain the perceived transformative learning experience students had two questions were presented to the participants. Question 7 was: "Below is a list of learning activities. Please indicate how frequently you think your instructors used each activity at the college by placing an 'X' in the appropriate box." There were nineteen instructional strategies set on a five-point Likert scale that were given for the participants to look at.

In question 8, the same nineteen instructional strategies, set on a four-point Likert scale were given to the participants. The participants were asked to indicate the extent they perceived each one of the instructional strategies influenced their perceived transformative learning experience.

Instructional Strategies and Frequency of Use

For the purpose of analysis, the frequency of "very frequently" and "frequently" scales were combined and reported as "VF/F" and the lower two scales "rarely" and "never" were reported together as "R/N" in table 12. The instructional strategies in table 12 are displayed with those that have the highest mean on top and progressively going down to the ones with the lowest mean. The four top-most frequently used instructional strategies are a lecture, mid-term and final exam, group presentation and summary, and reflection. A quick look at the top nine instructional strategies shows that the students' most frequent experience included taking exams, working on some form of assignments, lectures, and question and answer. A lesser frequency can be noticed in relation to out-of-classroom practical work and in-class student engagement.

Table 12. Frequency of Instructional Strategies

Response	N	M	SD	%VF/F	%SF	%R/N
Classroom lecture	136	4.63	.68	93.4	4.4	2.2
Mid and final examinations	137	4.59	.75	97.1	2.9	3.0
Group projects/assignments	137	4.10	.89	73.7	21.9	4.4
Summary/reflection assignments	137	4.03	1.00	70.8	21.9	7.3
Assigned reading assignments	137	3.98	1.14	73.0	13.1	13.8
Research papers	136	3.93	1.12	71.4	15.4	13.5
Group class presentation	137	3.88	.88	67.9	25.5	6.6
Question and answer	135	3.80	.99	62.2	31.1	6.7
Quiz on reading and lectures	136	3.80	1.25	69.9	14.7	15.5
Note-taking	136	3.68	1.05	59.6	27.2	13.1
Whole-class discussion	135	3.67	1.02	59.3	26.7	14.1
Small group discussions in class	135	3.67	1.04	58.5	27.4	14.1
Personal reflection	134	3.65	1.28	59.7	21.6	18.7
Homework/practice	136	3.60	1.15	55.9	23.5	20.5
Individual student class presentations	135	3.50	1.11	51.1	28.1	20.8
Demonstrations/ illustrations	134	3.25	1.14	41.8	33.6	27.7
Case studies in class	136	3.02	1.19	34.6	25	40.5
Practicum/internship	136	2.48	1.28	21.4	24.3	54.4
Field trip	137	2.18	1.21	13.9	20.4	65.7

Note: N=137; a five-point Likert scale was used (5 – very frequently, 4 – frequently, 3 – sometimes, 2 – rarely, and 1 – never).

Instructional Strategies and Influence

Question 8 of the instrument asked, "Below is a list of in-class and out-of-class learning activities. Please indicate to what extent each activity was influential in your transformative learning experience at the college by placing an 'X' in the box that accurately describes your experience."

Analysis of Findings

Table 13. Instructional Strategies and Their Perceived Influence

Response	N	M	SD	%VI	%SI	%S/N
Classroom lecture	137	3.81	0.43	82.5	16.1	1.5
Summary/reflection assignments	136	3.76	0.55	80.9	14.7	4.4
Mid and final examinations	137	3.68	0.59	74.5	19.0	6.6
Research papers	134	3.67	0.74	79.1	13.4	7.5
Group class presentation	135	3.58	0.67	67.4	23.7	8.9
Question and answer	136	3.57	0.74	69.1	22.1	8.8
Note-taking	136	3.56	0.70	65.4	27.2	7.4
Group projects/assignments	137	3.54	0.73	65.7	24.8	9.5
Assigned reading assignments	136	3.51	0.81	66.9	22.1	11.0
Small group discussions in class	136	3.49	0.78	62.5	27.2	10.3
Whole-class discussion	134	3.48	0.77	63.4	22.4	14.2
Personal reflection	135	3.44	0.94	67.4	16.3	16.3
Individual student class presentations	136	3.43	0.83	60.3	26.5	13.2
Quiz on reading and lectures	136	3.34	0.96	59.6	23.5	16.9
Homework/practice	134	3.34	0.93	59.7	21.6	18.7
Demonstrations/ illustrations	137	3.31	0.94	56.2	26.3	17.5
Case studies in class	136	3.18	0.96	47.1	32.4	20.6
Practicum/internship	132	2.76	1.24	40.9	20.5	38.6
Field trip	132	2.58	1.27	35.6	18.2	46.2

Note: N=137; the question used a four-point Likert scale of influence (4 – very influential, 3 – somewhat influential, 2 – slightly influential, and 1 – not influential at all). Slightly influential and not influential at all are reported together in this table.

The top three most influential instructional strategies (lectures, summary and reflections, and mid and final exams) in table 13, remained the same as those that were listed as being most frequent in table 12. The research Paper moved higher up indicating that the students perceived it to be influential. Another interesting observation was that note-taking also went higher. Although the frequency for note-taking was less, it was perceived to be an influential practice. One of the instructional strategies that moved further down on the list is group projects and assignments. Although it was one of the three most frequently used instructional strategies, it was shown to have a lesser influence on the students' perceived transformative learning experience. Overall, it can be observed that instructional strategies that required the students to be more engaged have moved higher up. Some of these strategies included question and answer, note-taking and small group discussions.

Pearson's correlation for relationship between the students' perceived influence of the instructional strategies and their perceived transformative learning scale was significant t (136) = .1946, r_{IsTl} = .437, p = .00. Pearson's correlation also indicated a significant relationship between the perceived influence of the instructional strategies and the subscales: awareness of need to change (r_{IsAn} = .254, p = .003), willingness to change (r_{IsWc} = .328, p = .00), reflective practice (r_{IsRp} = .412, p = .00), and integrative generation (r_{IsIg} = .400, p = .00).

A linear regression was used to test if the perceived influence of the instructional strategies significantly explained the perceived transformative learning experience scale. The results of the regression indicated the predictor explained 19.10 percent of the variance (R^2 = .191, F(1,135) = 31.80, p < .01) in the dependent variable. It was found that the students' perceived influence of instructional strategies significantly explained the perceived transformative learning experience (β = .33, p < .001). A p-value of less than .001 indicates that the null hypothesis that there is no statistically significant predictive relationship between perceived influential instructional strategies and transformative learning is rejected. Therefore, changes in the predictor's value are related to the changes in the response variable. A unit increase in the perceived influential instructional strategy will result in 0.33 increase of the dependent variable (perceived transformative learning).

Research Question 3

To what extent are there differences in the perceptions of the students and the teachers on the predictive relationship of the instructional strategies and perceived transformative learning experience?

Null Hypothesis 2

There is no statistically significant difference in the perceptions of the students and the teachers on the predictive relationship of the perceived transformative learning and the instructional strategies used within the ACTEA-related theological institutions.

In this section, the findings on the perceptions of the teachers on the frequency they used the different instructional strategies and the extent they believe each of the instructional strategies may have been influential to the students' transformative learning experiences are presented. Students' perspectives were already presented in the discussion of research question 2.

Table 14. Teachers' Perceptions of the Frequency of Use

Response	N	M	SD	%VF/F	%SF	%R/N
Classroom lecture	31	4.65	0.55	96.7	3.2	0
Assigned reading assignments	31	4.32	0.75	83.9	16.1	0.0
Mid and final examinations	31	4.10	1.04	80.6	9.7	9.7
Question and answer	31	4.06	0.77	80.6	16.1	3.2
Group projects/assignments	31	3.94	0.93	67.8	25.8	6.5
Note-taking	30	3.87	1.01	73.4	16.7	10.0
Demonstrations/ illustrations	31	3.77	0.84	64.7	29.0	6.5
Quiz on reading and lectures	31	3.74	1.09	54.9	35.5	9.7
Whole-class discussion	30	3.70	0.92	60.0	30.0	10.0
Research papers	28	3.68	0.98	66.1	35.7	7.1
Small group discussions in class	31	3.58	0.99	45.2	48.4	6.4
Personal reflection	31	3.48	0.81	41.9	51.6	6.5
Homework/practice	31	3.45	0.81	45.2	45.2	9.7
Summary/reflection assignments	31	3.42	0.85	45.2	41.9	12.9
Group class presentation	31	3.42	0.89	45.2	45.2	9.7
Individual student class presentations	31	3.29	0.82	38.8	45.2	16.1
Case studies in class	30	2.90	0.76	13.3	63.0	23.3
Practicum/internship	30	2.10	1.32	16.7	20.0	63.3
Field trip	30	2.00	0.87	6.7	6.7	76.7

Note: N=31; a five-point Likert scale was used (5 – very frequently, 4 – frequently, 3 – sometimes, 2 – rarely, and 1 – never). Very frequently and frequently are reported together and also rarely and never are reported together here.

The teachers were asked to indicate the frequency they used the different instructional strategies in their teaching. The question has the same nineteen instructional strategies that were set on a five-point Likert scale that was used in the students' survey. For the purpose of reporting, the frequency of the top two scales "very frequently" and "frequently" are combined and reported as "VF/F" and the lower "rarely" and "never" are reported together as "R/N" in table 14. The instructional strategies are re-ordered according to the obtained mean values from the one that has the highest mean value to the one that has the lowest.

In table 15, a comparison of the perceptions of the teachers and the students on the frequency they used each of the instructional strategies is presented. Of the ten most frequently used instructional strategies eight are mentioned by both groups to be most frequent. From among the ones where they differ, the teachers' perception of the whole-class discussion (M=3.70) is very close to that of the students' perception of it (3.67). The teachers' perception on the use of demonstration was much higher than the students' and the students' perception on the use of group presentation and summary/reflection assignment was much higher than that of the teachers.

Table 15. Comparison of the Frequency of Use

No	Response	Teachers				Students			
		N	M	SD	%	N	M	SD	%
1	Question and answer	31	4.06	0.77	80.6	135	3.80	.99	62.2
2	Classroom lecture	31	4.65	0.55	96.7	136	4.63	.68	93.4
3	Demonstrations/ illustrations	31	3.77	0.84	64.7	134	3.25	1.14	41.8
4	Group projects/ assignments	31	3.94	0.93	67.8	137	4.10	.89	73.7
5	Research papers	28	3.68	0.98	66.1	136	3.93	1.12	71.4
6	Assigned reading assignments	31	4.32	0.75	83.9	137	3.98	1.14	73.0
7	Individual student class presentations	31	3.29	0.82	38.8	135	3.50	1.11	51.1

Analysis of Findings

No	Response	Teachers				Students			
		N	M	SD	%	N	M	SD	%
8	Case studies in class	30	2.90	0.76	13.3	136	3.02	1.19	34.6
9	Small group discussions in class	31	3.58	0.99	45.2	135	3.67	1.04	58.5
10	Personal reflection	31	3.48	0.81	41.9	134	3.65	1.28	59.7
11	Quiz on reading and lectures	31	**3.74**	1.09	54.9	136	**3.80**	1.25	69.9
12	Mid and final examinations	31	**4.10**	1.04	80.6	137	**4.59**	.75	97.1
13	Field trip	30	2.00	0.87	6.7	137	2.18	1.21	13.9
14	Homework/practice	31	3.45	0.81	45.2	136	3.60	1.15	55.9
15	Note-taking	30	**3.87**	1.01	73.4	136	**3.68**	1.05	59.6
16	Whole-class discussion	30	**3.70**	0.92	60.1	135	3.67	1.02	59.3
17	Group class presentation	31	3.42	0.89	45.2	137	**3.88**	.88	67.9
18	Summary/reflection assignments	31	3.42	0.85	45.2	137	**4.03**	1.00	70.8
19	Practicum/ internship	30	2.10	1.32	16.7	136	2.48	1.28	21.4

Note: N = 31 for teachers and N = 137 for students. The top ten most frequent instructional strategies reported by both groups are in bold. The items are ordered according to the order on the survey.

A test was carried out to determine the presence of a statistically significant difference in the perception of the top ten most frequently used instructional strategies between the teachers and the students. A t-test for independent groups yielded that the perception of the teachers (M = 3.98, SD = .10, n = 10) was not statistically significant from the perception of the students (M = 4.04, SD = .10, n=10) at t(18) = 2.10, p = .63 (2 tail).

Influence of Instructional Strategies

A question was asked of the teachers to indicate their perception of the extent each of the instructional strategies is influential in the transformative learning experiences students had at the college. This question used a four-point Likert scale of influence (4 – very influential, 3 – somewhat influential, 2 – slightly influential, and 1 – not influential at all). The scales, "slightly influential" and "not influential at all" are reported together in table 16 as "S/N."

The instructional strategies that the teachers perceived to be most influential appeared to be different from the instructional strategies both the teachers and students reported to be most frequent. The top five strategies reported as being most influential were: demonstration and illustration, question and answer, group class presentation, research papers, and individual class presentation. The lecture came in sixth place. Instructional strategies that were related to exams appeared to be perceived to have less influence on students' transformative learning experience.

Table 16. Teachers Perception of the Influence of Each of the Instructional Strategies

Response	N	M	SD	%VI	%SI	%S/N
Demonstrations/ illustrations	30	3.73	0.58	73.3	23.3	3.3
Question and answer	31	3.58	0.67	61.3	32.3	6.5
Group class presentation	31	3.48	0.63	54.8	38.7	16.1
Research papers	30	3.43	0.68	46.7	46.7	6.7
Individual student class presentations	30	3.37	0.61	43.3	50.0	6.7
Classroom lecture	31	3.35	0.66	38.7	54.8	6.5
Small group discussions in class	31	3.35	0.61	41.9	51.6	6.5
Group projects/assignments	31	3.32	0.75	41.9	45.2	12.9
Whole-class discussion	31	3.32	0.60	38.7	54.8	6.5
Note-taking	30	3.30	0.79	43.3	40.0	16.7
Summary/reflection assignments	31	3.29	0.74	45.2	38.7	16.1
Case studies in class	30	3.27	0.94	50.0	26.7	23.3
Personal reflection	31	3.23	0.72	38.7	45.2	16.1
Assigned reading assignments	31	3.16	0.64	29.0	58.1	12.9

Analysis of Findings

Response	N	M	SD	%VI	%SI	%S/N
Quiz on reading and lectures	30	3.10	0.88	36.7	33.3	30.0
Homework/practice	31	3.10	0.75	32.3	45.2	22.6
Mid and final examinations	30	3.03	0.85	33.3	40.0	26.6
Practicum/internship	30	3.03	1.03	36.7	36.7	26.7
Field trip	30	2.77	1.04	30.0	30.0	40.0

Note: N = 31 for teachers and N = 137 for students.

Table 17 provides a comparison of the perceptions of the teachers and students on the extent each of the instructional strategies was influential in the transformative learning experiences of the students.

Table 17. Influence Comparison

		Teachers				Students			
No	Response	N	M	SD	%	N	M	SD	%
1	Question and answer	31	**3.58**	0.67	61.3	136	**3.57**	0.74	69.1
2	Classroom lecture	31	**3.35**	0.66	38.7	137	**3.81**	0.43	82.5
3	Demonstrations/ illustrations	30	**3.73**	0.58	73.7	137	3.31	0.94	56.2
4	Group projects/ assignments	31	**3.32**	0.75	41.9	137	**3.54**	0.73	65.7
5	Research papers	30	**3.43**	0.68	46.7	134	**3.67**	0.74	79.1
6	Assigned reading assignments	31	3.16	0.64	29.0	136	**3.51**	0.81	66.9
7	Individual student class presentations	30	**3.37**	0.61	43.3	136	3.43	0.83	60.3
8	Case studies in class	30	3.27	0.94	50.0	136	3.18	0.96	47.1
9	Small group discussions in class	31	**3.35**	0.61	41.9	136	**3.49**	0.78	62.5
10	Personal reflection	31	3.23	0.72	38.7	135	3.44	0.94	67.4
11	Quiz on reading and lectures	30	3.10	0.88	36.7	136	3.34	0.96	59.6

		Teachers				Students			
No	Response	N	M	SD	%	N	M	SD	%
12	Mid and final examinations	30	3.03	0.85	33.3	137	**3.68**	0.59	74.5
13	Field trip	30	2.77	1.04	30.0	132	2.58	1.27	35.6
14	Homework/practice	31	3.10	0.75	32.3	134	3.34	0.93	59.7
15	Note-taking	30	**3.30**	0.79	43.3	136	**3.56**	0.70	65.4
16	Whole-class discussion	31	**3.32**	0.60	38.7	134	3.48	0.77	63.7
17	Group class presentation	31	**3.48**	0.63	54.8	135	**3.58**	0.67	67.4
18	Summary/reflection assignments	31	3.29	0.74	45.2	136	**3.76**	0.55	80.9
19	Practicum/internship	30	3.03	1.03	36.7	132	2.76	1.24	40.9

Note: The top ten perceived most influential instructional strategies are in bold. The percentage given here is only the "very influential" scale. The items are ordered according to the order on the instrument.

Of the ten most influential instructional strategies seven were mentioned by both groups as being influential to students' transformative learning experience. However, while a great number of the students were perceiving lecture, mid and final exams, and summary and reflection very highly, the teachers perceived them to have a lesser influence. The teachers perceived question and answer, small group discussions, whole-class discussions to be more influential to students' transformative learning experience.

A t-test for two independent samples was carried out to determine the presence of a statistically significant difference in the perception of the top ten most influential instructional strategies between the teachers and the students. The test showed that the difference between the perception of the teachers (M = 3.42, SD = .04, n = 10) and that of the students (M = 3.62, SD = .03, n=10) was statistically significant, $t(18) = 2.10$, $p = .00$ (2-tail).

Focus Group Findings – Instructional Strategies

Each of the instructional strategies that were included in the survey was discussed in the focus groups for the extent they were used and the extent they were perceived to be valuable to the students' transformative learning experience. The discussion provided some important clarification on some of the instructional strategies. A summary of what the students said in regard to each of the instructional strategies is presented as follows.

Question and answer. Students believe that teachers used the question-and-answer method in the class. However, its use was limited, and they would like to see it being used more. It was limited by the teacher's desire to finish the portion they planned for the day. It was also limited by the fact that it usually came towards the end of class. They suggested for it to be included at different times of the class, giving opportunities for students to ask questions. The following were some of the reasons offered for having the question-and-answer method more frequently.

- The absence of question and answer makes the process a one-way process, and that is not education.
- The ability to ask questions allows us to listen attentively.
- It encourages students to come to class having read the assigned readings.
- Students learn from other students as they answer questions.
- A teacher also has an opportunity to learn from students.
- Questions make teachers come to class better prepared.

Lectures. The students felt that mostly the teachers spoke throughout the class period with occasional questions and class discussions. The students suggested that the teacher should engage the students more in the process of learning. A participant from C3 said that "students who are not engaged in the learning process would end up only preparing for an exam." Another participant from C5 said, "You may have been listening for some time but then you get tired and your ability to listen reduces. However, if you are active, sometimes you will not know how quick the time goes." The groups believe that one cannot get away without a lecture, but they suggested the following modifications in the use of the lecture method in class.

- The lecture should be shortened and used in combination with question and answer, discussion, personal reflection, case studies, and other teaching methods.
- Active learning must be encouraged by having students participate during a lecture – small group discussions and allowing students to share their experiences should be encouraged.
- By giving students an opportunity to reflect on their readings and share in class, students will be encouraged to read reflectively.
- The design of the lecture must fit the diversity of backgrounds of the students and how different students learn. It should, therefore, take into consideration all the members of the class and not only one or two students who seem to understand. This need to differentiate among the students was articulated very well by a participant from C2 who said,

  > When a teacher lectures, it is to help the students learn. So, what the teacher does in class to explain things should take this into consideration. It begins with knowing the students. The lecture should be there but how should it be done is an important question. A lecture I do not understand is not helpful. Among us, there are many presidents of synods, teachers, those who have completed twelfth grade of school and many others. The lecture system should be one that takes all this diversity into consideration. The way they teach must fit the backgrounds of the students.

- In lecturing, teachers should take time to explain instead of reading, maintain eye contact with students and regularly check for student understanding.

Demonstration and illustration. Some teachers used demonstration and illustration in their classes. The students found it to be helpful to understand difficult concepts. They believe it would work more with some courses than others. They would like to see more teachers use them.

Group projects/assignments. All the groups from the five colleges indicated that group projects and assignments were used frequently in their institutions. However, they had mixed responses to the method. They noted that in using the method,

- Weaker students can be helped to learn in groups,
- there are times when the students can be better teachers, and
- when all participate, they can learn things from others.

However, a number of participants in the groups have noted that,
- students are not at a level to effectively use this method,
- many do not work and they hide behind the work of others,
- students miss out on their learning and suffer from not participating in group work, and
- it promotes laziness as some students get the grades without working.

All the groups were strongly suggesting getting rid of group projects and assignments or reduce their use significantly. A participant from C2 expressed it is emphatically by saying,

> When we are asked to work in groups and submit an assignment, I have not seen a healthy group work done in my life. One or two people always do it. So, I do not encourage that method. I think the possibility for it to benefit the group members is weak. That is the way I have seen it and continues to be that way. It is because that is our nature as humans.

Where the method is used, the groups suggested that:
- The teacher should select the members of the groups.
- The teacher should tell the groups that they will arbitrarily choose a student to present in order to encourage each student to prepare. "If presenters are selected randomly, we may exclude students who do not work, from joining the group in the future" (C3).
- A system should be established to follow-up on students who do not participate.

Research papers. Three of the five colleges (C1, C4, and C5) have indicated that research papers were used as an instructional strategy in their institutions as part of the course assignments. They all agreed that they would like to see it being used more frequently. One of the colleges (C2), indicated that students work on research papers as part of their graduation requirements and not as part of the requirements in the individual courses. But they would like to see it being used in the individual courses. On the other hand, a participant from C5 indicated that it is being used, but they would rather not have it since the grading of such assignments is subjective, and they would rather have exams that are more objective than doing research papers.

Generally, all the colleges agree on the value of having research papers and would like to see it being used more frequently. They mentioned the following as the advantages of using research papers as an instructional strategy.

- It draws out students' potential; and their writing skill develops.
- Good preparation for those who seek to do further studies on a graduate level.
- Things you learn on your own are enjoyable.
- It helps to reflect, read, and know.

Reading assignments. All colleges indicated that reading assignments were used as instructional strategies. They indicated that they helped them be better prepared for class. However, one of the students said that "they teach students lying" (C1) as the students end up reporting what they have not read. The groups generally encourage that reading assignments should be used but they need to be proportional to the course load requirement and teachers should implement a clear follow-up system to assess students' reading.

Individual presentation. Four of the colleges (C1, C2, C3, and C4) indicated that students did individual class presentations in some of the courses. They believe that it helped them develop the skill and confidence in public speaking (C2). One of the colleges indicated that students do not do individual class presentations, but it would help to have it. It was pointed out that it would work only in classes where the class size is small (C1).

Case studies. All the groups from the five colleges indicated that very few teachers used case studies in their colleges. They all suggested for it to be used by more teachers. One of the colleges indicated that it would be a helpful tool to contextualize what they learned and come up with solutions to real life situations in their churches (C1).

Small group discussion. Four of the five colleges indicated that teachers used small group discussions in class as an instructional tool. One of the colleges (C5) indicated that they have not had small group discussions in class. A participant from this college said,

Teachers do not break students into small groups for discussions. Mostly, it is a lecture that we have. It will be extremely helpful if there are small group discussions. Sometimes the class hour is short, and it may be difficult to have small group discussions. However, it would be good if there was a small group discussion. It will be good if there is less of a lecture method and instead of the teacher covering the whole book if they provide the main points and decides where the students can discuss, and the teacher comes back to give a conclusion at the end.

All five colleges felt that small group discussion would be a helpful tool to engage students in their learning under the oversight of the teacher. It would also provide opportunities for students to learn from others. They would all like to see more teachers using this method.

Personal reflection. Only one of the colleges indicated that teachers used personal reflection in class as a teaching tool. Although students were individually engaged in a personal reflection in class, the teachers did not include that as part of the learning tools. All the groups agreed that an intentionally planned engagement of students in personal reflection would be good.

Quizzes, mid-term and final exams. All the groups indicated that they have quizzes, mid-term and final exams. They all agreed that the right number of quizzes would make students maintain their reading and work on their studies. One of the groups (C4) indicated that it also helps students have an idea of the type of questions they can expect for final exams. All groups have indicated that they would like to continue to have quizzes.

While three of the colleges agreed that they would like to see final exams continue to be there, two of the colleges voiced their concern that final exams only encouraged the memorization of content. The two colleges suggested that the content memorized for final exams were forgotten soon after the exams were done (C1). They suggested that final exams should not be given, or their use be reduced. One student from C4 commented that students who are naturally able to memorize prefer to have final exams but those who prefer writing and reading may prefer writing research papers instead of doing a final exam.

Field trips. Two of the colleges (C3 and C4) indicated that they had field trips and three of the colleges indicated that they had no field trips. All groups agreed that field trips would help them build relationships but also would give them exposure to other experiences.

Note-taking. All the groups agreed that note-taking is important and there were many students who took notes and yet there were others who did not take notes and they relied on the handouts they received from the teachers. One of the participants from C1 said, "students do not take notes – teachers should follow-up with the students to see if they are taking notes." On the other hand, a student from C3 said that all students take notes. They went on to explain that there are some who may be in the college for the grades and they would just wait for the notes from the teachers and they will just memorize that in preparation for the exam. Some teachers use PowerPoint presentations and promise to give notes. Therefore, students may not be encouraged to take notes. The groups agree that the students must be encouraged to take notes in class.

Homework. Four of the groups agreed that homework was given at different times by different teachers and it is necessary to have. One of the groups did not mention homework as a method to have in class.

Whole-class discussions. It was occasionally that teachers planned for a whole-class discussion. When they did, students learned from the experiences and opinions of other students. There were times when the questions that were raised in class ended up becoming a class discussion and students have appreciated those times. Two of the colleges (C3 and C5) did not mention this as a method to use.

Summary and reflection. The teachers in all five colleges used summary and reflections on the reading assignments students were given. They all believed that it is an important method of teaching and suggest continuing using it.

Practicum/internship. Except for one of the colleges (C5), all colleges had practicums. One of the four colleges (C2) suggested that the practicums should be required for the students who were not involved in church ministry. Another of the four colleges (C1) suggested that it should have a close follow-up since some students falsely report that they have completed the practicum. All of the five colleges agree on its value to help students apply what they are learning.

Explaining the Quantitative Data Using the Qualitative Finding

It will be helpful here to note a few of the points where the qualitative data collected through the focus group clarified the data that was collected through the quantitative method. Four of the most important ones will be briefly shared as follows.

The first one is in relation to the lecture method. The lecture method is reported as the most frequent and most influential instructional strategy by the students. The focus group data does confirm that as well. However, it clarifies that the usefulness of the lecture method is determined by the extent it engages the students in the learning process. This is best done by using the lecture method in combination with other instructional strategies such as small groups, question and answer, whole-class discussion, personal reflection, etc.

The second instructional strategy to consider is group projects and assignments. It is reported by the students as the third most frequent and one of the top ten most influential instructional strategies. However, the focus group data indicates that although the method is valuable, the students believe that its use has not been very fruitful. It has instead been causing harm to some students who were allowing others to do the work and they themselves were not engaged in the learning. A number of the groups have indicated that this instructional strategy should not be used, or its use be reduced. Where it is used, the groups suggest that certain important measures be taken to ensure members of the groups are engaged in the work.

The focus group data also sheds light on the understanding of the finding on quizzes and final exams. The quantitative results indicated that quizzes are one of the top ten frequently used instructional strategy, but it has dropped off the list of the top ten most influential instructional strategy both from the perception of the teachers as well as the students. However, the focus group indicated that the students actually would like to see quizzes to be used regularly to help them keep up with their readings of the course material they are learning. On the other hand, they believe final exams encourage memorization for the exam. Two of the colleges believe that final exams do not contribute much to students' transformative learning experience and hence should not be used, or their use is reduced. It was preferred by one group from one college because it allowed for objective grading of the work in comparison to a research paper.

Finally, note-taking is in the top ten of the most frequent and most influential instructional strategies. The focus group data confirms its important influence on learning, but it also indicates that it is a method that many of the students are not taking advantage of. The reason that was given for this is that the students are waiting to receive the lecture notes from the teachers, and they use that to prepare for the exams. The focus tends to be prepared for exams rather than learning for transformative learning experience.

Classroom Observation

Classroom observation was done at each of the five colleges. The purpose of this observation was to determine the different instructional strategies that were used by teachers in the colleges and the ways the students were engaged in the classrooms. A summary of the instructional strategies that were used and the ways the students were engaged in the classes will be presented.

The instructional strategies that were used between the five colleges during the time the researcher did the observations included: question and answer, "pair and share," lectures, note-taking, illustration, whole-class discussion, PowerPoint, black/whiteboard. The frequency each of these methods was used between the five colleges is summarized in table 18.

Table 18. Instructional Strategies Used during Observation

Instructional Strategy	No. of Classes That Used	%
Lecture	9	100
Question and answer	9	100
Pair and share (small group)	2	22
Illustration	7	78
Whole-class discussion	4	44
Note-taking	9	100
Class notes	3	33
PowerPoint	3	33
Black/whiteboard	9	100

As indicated in table 18, all classes used the lecture, question and answer, the blackboard, and students were also taking notes. The degree to which each one was happening was, however, different. The different methods were used to different degrees in the different classes. Three of the classes had pair and share and whole-class discussions as the major instructional strategy where there was much lesser amount of time given for lecture. The teachers in these classes took between five to ten minutes to explain a concept and then would give the class another activity to work in groups or discuss as a class. In four of the classes, the teachers had a lecture that had a clear structure to follow, they took time to explain, they paused at different times to check for understanding of the lecture, and they also allowed students to ask questions. The primary instructional strategy was lecture, but they were explaining, asking questions, and allowing for student inputs at different times.

All the teachers gave time for students to ask questions during class. There were a couple of classes where students were neither answering nor asking questions. In one of the classes, the teacher switched between two languages to help students understand certain concepts that they felt the students may not have understood. Since the primary language of instruction was English, and the language competency of some of the students was limited, students may have struggled to express themselves with confidence and hence chose to remain silent.

There was a second class where students were also neither asking nor answering questions. The teacher was switching between the two languages. However, the class continued to be silent. When the teacher did not get much response from the students, the teacher told the class a story about a teacher who asked his students if they were confused and when they responded to him affirmatively, he told them that he was successful. The researcher suspects that the teacher told this story because he felt the students did not understand the concept that he taught. The teacher did not attempt to explain the concepts again and the class was finished with that.

In the class where the teacher chose to speak purely in English, the students were silent throughout the class time. However, in the other class where the teacher was switching between the languages, the students were more open, and they were discussing. It is possible to consider the possibility that students may not ask or answer questions in class due to the language barrier or possibly a lack of clarity on the subject matter that is taught.

Student-teacher interactions appeared to be different depending on the degree the teachers engaged the students in the class. Some had the class discussions, others had the small group discussions in pairs, others had the openness to have students ask and they would also regularly check for student understanding of their lecture. In the classes where pair and share or the whole-class discussion method was used, the dynamics of the classes were lively, and the students appeared to have a good relationship with the teachers and among themselves. It allowed the students to voice their opinions and feel comfortable to do so in class. In a couple of the classes where the class discussion and the pair and share were happening, students at one point were debating an idea across the room.

Research Question 4

To what extent do student interactions with other individuals in the college predict or explain self-reported transformative learning experience in students studying at the ACTEA-related theological colleges in Ethiopia?

Null Hypothesis 3

There is no statistically significant relationship between the students' perceived transformative learning and their interactions with other individuals within the college.

Student Perceptions of Influential Relationships

This section presents the perceived influence of interpersonal relationships on the students' transformative learning experience. The perceptions of both the students and the teachers are presented and any similarity or difference between the two groups is explored in a separate table.

The mean values for the influences of the teachers, the students, and administrative staff were all above 3.0 (see table 19), which is an indication of agreement to the presence of influence on students' transformative learning experience. It is worth noting that the students', as well as the teachers' influences, were very close to each other. The teachers' influence out of class and the influence of the administrative staff is rated lowest.

Table 19. Student Perception of Influential Relationships

No	Response	n	M	SD	% of Agreement
1	Teachers' effort to form relationship with students in the classroom	137	3.29	0.78	89.0
2	Teachers' effort to form relationship with students outside of classroom	137	3.01	0.84	75.9
3	Teachers' effort to see students learn	137	3.34	0.72	91.3
4	Teachers' modeling	136	3.46	0.73	92.0
5	Opportunities to interact with students in-class	137	3.42	0.70	93.4
6	Opportunities to interact with students out-of-class	137	3.34	0.69	93.4
7	Administrative staff approach to students	137	3.04	0.90	78.1

N = 137. A four-point Likert scale was used (4 – strongly agree, 3 – agree, 2 – disagree, and 1 – strongly disagree). For reporting purposes only, the agreement (strongly agree and agree) are reported. The remaining percentage is to disagree and strongly disagree.

In order to confirm the students' responses in item four, a separate item (question 5) was included which asked the participants to respond with a "yes" or "no." The question was stated as "Were there teachers, or students, or administrators who had an influence on the change you experienced while you were studying at the college?" Their responses showed that for n = 125, 92.2 percent of them responded affirmatively and the remaining 7.8 percent responded with a "no" indicating that they did not feel that their transformative learning experience was influenced by any of the interpersonal relationships they had with the teachers, students, or administrative staff at the college.

The teachers were also asked to rate the extent the students' interpersonal relationships with the teachers, students, and administrative staff may have influenced the students' transformative learning experience. Their response is presented in table 20. An important difference that can be noted in comparing the teachers' response to that of the students' response is that the administrative staff are perceived to have a much higher influence on students (96.5 percent) than what was perceived by the students (78.1 pecent).

Table 20. Teachers' Perception of Influential Relationships

No	Response	n	M	SD	% of Agreement
1	Teachers' effort to form relationship with students in the classroom	29	3.45	0.51	100
2	Teachers' effort to form relationship with students outside of classroom	28	3.14	0.71	82.1
3	Teachers' effort to see students learn	28	3.46	0.69	89.2
4	Teachers' modeling	29	3.34	0.72	93.1
5	Opportunities to interact with students in-class	29	3.24	0.64	89.7
6	Opportunities to interact with students out-of-class	29	3.31	0.60	93.1
7	Administrative staff approach to students	29	3.21	0.49	96.5

N = 31. A four-point Likert scale was used (4 – strongly agree, 3 – agree, 2 – disagree, and 1 – strongly disagree). For reporting purposes only, the agreement (agree and strongly disagree) is reported. The remaining percentage is to disagree and strongly disagree.

The students' perception of the influence of the interpersonal relationships on their perceived transformative learning experience (M = 3.27, SD = 0.07, n = 7) was compared to that of the teachers' (M = 3.31, SD = 0.05, n = 7) for any difference between them. The difference was not statistically significant t(12) = 2.18, p = .67 (2-tail).

Since a large number of the students perceived to have been influenced by an interpersonal relationship while studying at the college, item six asked the participants to give examples of how others were able to have an influence on them. The participants gave examples of how they were influenced by the teachers, the students, and the administrative staff. These influences were grouped into seven categories. A count of the number of participants that mentioned an influence from each category is indicated in table 21. A large percent of these examples was related to the influence of the teachers.

Table 21. Perceived Influences Due to Interpersonal Relationships

Response	Frequency n = 95	%
Teachers' exemplary life	54	56.8
Teachers' approach to students	43	45.3
Teachers' approach to teaching	42	44.2
Students' exemplary life	8	8.4
Students' care for each other	7	7.4
Time together with other students	8	8.4
Relationship with administrative staff	1	1.1

Note: N = 137

Although the examples that are given here for the influence of the students is much lower than that which was given for the teachers, the influence of the students is indicated to be high in table 19.

A blockwise multiple regression analysis on the extent students' interpersonal relationship with the teachers and administrators and other students accounts for the variance in the perceived student transformative learning experience was carried out. Model one indicated that the interpersonal relationship with teachers explained 23.3 percent of the perceived transformative learning experience ($R^2 = .233$, $F(1.135) = 40.96$, $p < .01$). It was found that interpersonal relationships with teachers significantly predicted the perceived transformative learning experiences ($\beta = .265$, $p < .01$). In model two, the R^2 change was 4.9 percent at $p < .01$. This indicated that the interpersonal relationship with other students explained 4.9 percent of the variance in the students' perceived transformative learning experience. There was an F value associated with the whole model ($F(2,134) = .263$, $p < .01$) accounting for 28.2 percent of the variance. In the whole model, it was found that interpersonal relationships with teachers and administrative staff significantly predicted transformative learning experience ($\beta = .186$, $p < .01$) as did the interpersonal relationship with other students ($\beta = .145$, $p < .01$).

Focus Group Findings – Interpersonal Relationships

The groups were asked the question – what are the different ways teachers influence students' transformative learning experiences? The responses of the groups from all five institutions were put into four categories – teachers' in-class interaction with students, teachers' effort in students' learning, out of class teachers' interaction with students, and teachers' exemplary life. An explanation of the main factors related to each of the categories and their relationship to the obtained quantitative data is presented as follows.

Teachers' in-class interaction with students. The groups indicated that teachers were able to influence students when they recognized student differences and were able to engage each of the students in the class. A participant from C2 explained that the teachers must recognize the students' differences and engage them accordingly. They explained this saying, "there are students who answer right away and there are those who take time in answering. If a teacher does not know these things a teacher is not a teacher." They also influenced students just by the fact that they remembered students' names and were able to help the students when they needed help. As much as the teachers were able to influence students positively, the groups also pointed out that students' transformative learning experience can be negatively affected through inappropriate treatment of students and by the manner they responded to questions in class. A student from C1 said,

> The character teachers demonstrate can create a gap with students. The manner we answer questions in the class shows what kind of heart we have for the students, why we teach. Sometimes students come to class having sacrificed so much and yet, there are teachers who do not even put a notice saying the class is canceled. This affects students' relationships. . . . The relationship students have with teachers is key.

Teachers' effort in students' learning. Teachers were able to influence students as they paid attention to students' learning and were willing to offer help when needed. They influenced students by recognizing that they are able to reach into areas they themselves could not, by investing in the lives of the students everything they could. A student from C2 stated this so well as follows,

We should be looking at it from the gospel perspective because, in this school, the school is meant to be shaping people in preparing others to reach into places where the school itself will not be able to reach. This has not been given sufficient attention. If I am living here in Addis Ababa, and we have men and women who suffer in serving God at the border of the country and have come here to study with us, they should be shaped and appreciated and encouraged for the work they are doing. There are a lot of them who are facing the sword and are being stoned for the work of the gospel. Let alone out there, even here in Addis Ababa, when we go out to do evangelism, people throw stones at us, bring dirt and put it into our mouth. There are many who go into places where I cannot reach. Teachers need to be adjusted very much in their attitude of teaching. These students can be slaughtered, they can be killed, they can be burned. Teaching should not be seen only from grades perspective. It should not be seen from income perspective. I think there should be some work that needs to be done on the teachers.

Out of class teachers' interaction with students. The teachers' willingness to serve students, visiting them at home when they were sick, spending time with students over tea, and share their lives and ask how students were doing or spend some time praying for them had an influence on the students' transformative learning experience. Students were greatly influenced by teachers who were able to notice that a student was struggling and offered to help.

Teachers' exemplary life. The exemplary life of the teachers was mentioned as being influential in students' transformative learning experience. The demonstration of this included such things as attending chapel with the students and serving in the chapel. But it also included just the way they lived, which the students observed. A participant from C1, in explaining the need to be exposed to the lives of the teachers said, "we will be able to share the life that is with them. Life teaches us. We will be able to see what challenges they go through."

While the teachers were affirmed as being influential in the transformative learning experiences the students had, they also mentioned that students may also be negatively impacted by the character the teacher displays. Almost all the groups have mentioned that teachers are mostly not found in the company of students outside of class. One of the participants from C5 said,

> You would want the teachers to come and encourage you, but what you see is the teacher teach and just leave. What I would want is to have the teachers having tea with me during break time. They do not even eat lunch together. So where is the relationship coming from? If we ate together and had time to talk, I believe the relationship would build.

A participant from C2 acknowledged that there were teachers who noticed students struggling and offered to help but "there are others who do not even come close to the students and talk to them." Another participant from C4 said,

> I think it will be good if teachers spend more time with students in the chapel and have tea with us. We have teachers who have a lot of experience in ministry. They are very well-known people and if we get to spend time with them outside of class, we will learn a lot from their life and ministry experiences.

The groups acknowledged the influence the teachers had on their transformative learning experience, but they were also saying that the opportunities to do that have not been sufficiently utilized. This was also well reflected in the quantitative data where there was an 89 percent (M = 3.29) agreement to teachers' in-class influence and 75.9 percent (M = 3.1) outside of class influence. The teachers' perception of the influence they had on students outside of class seems to also be relatively lower (82.1 percent, M = 3.29) as compared to their in-class influence of (100 percent agreement).

Influence of student-student interpersonal relationship

All groups agreed that there were both positive and negative student influences at the colleges. The influencing characteristics mentioned in all the groups were grouped into three categories: in-class interaction with students, out of class interactions, and exemplary life of the students.

In-class interaction with students. The opportunities students had to interact with each other through the group work assignments they did or the small group discussion they had in class, had given them opportunities to learn from the experiences of other students.

Out of class interaction with students. The times that students got together in prayer and reading the Bible outside of class and the opportunity for them to serve together had been mentioned as being influential for them. As a participant from C2 mentioned, the system of caring for students in need, which the college established, had also given students the opportunities to have an influence on others.

Exemplary life of students. The students came from diverse backgrounds and diverse ministry experiences and the college had given them the opportunity to learn from others. A participant from C3 said, "There are students who are older and have been in ministry for a while. There are diverse experiences which have been influential." A student from C4 said, "we learn from those who have exemplary lifestyles and experiences."

Although all the participants have indicated that there were both positive and negative influences and they have been able to give examples of ways students were able to influence others, one participant from C5 said, "I have not been influenced by any of the students here. The pastors themselves need pastors." The quantitative data has indicated a 93.4 percent agreement of students' influence on the transformative learning experiences of students. This indicates that there were some who did not have that experience of being influenced positively by other students.

Research Question 5

To what extent is the self-reported transformative learning experience of students in full-time study different from those in part-time studies?

Null Hypothesis 4

There is no statistically significant difference between students in part-time studies and those in full-time studies in their perceived transformative learning experience.

Item ten asked the participants to choose one that best described their enrollment at the college. In their response (n=132) 71.2 percent indicated that they were enrolled full-time at the college. Another 8.3 percent indicated that they were enrolled full-time at the college while studying or working part-time at a different place. That adds up to a total of 79.5 percent who were enrolled full-time. The remaining 20.5 percent indicated that they were enrolled at the college part-time while having either a full-time or part-time engagement.

The perceived students' transformative learning experience between students in the part-time study and those in the full-time study were not significantly correlated, r = .074, p < .05. A t-test for independent samples was carried was also out to test for a significant difference in the perceived transformative learning experience between the students in their part-time studies (M = 3.65, SD = .28) and those in full-time studies (M = 3.58, SD = .38). The difference was not statistically significant, t (132) = 1.96, p = .596.

Multiple Regression Analysis with Three IVs

It has already been shown that the students' perceived influence of the instructional strategies as well as the students' interpersonal relationships with teachers and administrative staff and with other students were significant predictors of transformative learning. This section seeks to determine the extent to which interpersonal relationships account for the variance over and above the perceived influence of the instructional strategies. This is done in relation to the overall perception of the transformative learning scale and also the four subscales in order to determine if their influence will be different at different levels of the transformation.

In relation to the overall transformative learning scale, model one showed that perceived influence of the instructional strategies explained 19.1 percent of the variance (R^2 = .191, F (1,135) = 31.8 at p < .01). This showed that the influence of instructional strategies significantly predicted the transformative learning experience of the students (β = .327, p < .01). In model two, the interpersonal relationship has an R^2 change of .127 with an F Change of 12.36 at p < .01. This indicates that the 12.36 percent change is statistically significant. The F value (F (3,133) = 20.63, p< .01) associated with the whole model (R^2 = 31.8%) accounted for 31.8 percent of the variance. It was found that the perceived influence of instruction strategies was a significant predictor of transformative learning experience (β = .167, p < .01) as did the interpersonal relationship with teacher and administrative staff (β = .157, p < .001) and other students (β = .101, p < .05).

The blockwise regression analysis for the "awareness of the need to change" indicated that in model one, the perceived influence of instruction strategies accounted for 4.7 percent of the variance ($R2 = .064$, $F(1,135) = 9.29$, $p < .01$). It was found that instructional strategy was a significant predictor of awareness of the need to change ($\beta = .214$, $p < .01$). However, model two showed that interpersonal relationships were not significant predictors of awareness of need to change with an R^2 change of .027, $p > .05$. The interpersonal relationship with teachers was not significant ($\beta = .078$, $p > .05$) nor was the interpersonal relationship with students ($\beta = .057$, $p > .05$).

A similar analysis was done with regard to the "willingness to change" variable. It was determined that in model one, the perceived influence of the instruction strategies accounted for 10.8 percent of the variance ($R^2 = .108$, $F(1,135) = 16.3$, $p < .01$). It was found that instructional strategy was a significant predictor of willingness to change ($\beta = .268$, $p < .01$). Model two showed that interpersonal relationships were significant predictors of "willingness to change" with an R^2 change of .078 at $p < .01$. The interpersonal relationship with teachers was not a significant predictor ($\beta = .055$, $p > .05$). However, the interpersonal relationship with students was significant ($\beta = .160$, $p < .01$).

The analysis in relation to the variable "reflective practice" showed that in model one the perceived influence of the instruction strategies accounted for 16.9 percent of the variance ($R2 = .169$, $F(1,135) = 27.5$, $p < .01$). It was found that instructional strategy was a significant predictor of reflective practice ($\beta = .375$, $p < .01$). Model two showed that interpersonal relationships were significant predictors of "reflective practice," with an R^2 change of .086, $p < .01$. The interpersonal relationship with teachers was significant ($\beta = .176$, $p < .01$). However, the interpersonal relationship with students was not significant ($\beta = .076$, $p > .05$).

Finally, the analysis related to the "integrative generation" showed that in model one, the perceived influence of the instructional strategies accounted for 16 percent of the variance ($R^2 = .160$, $F(1,135) = 25.76$, $p < .01$). It was found that instructional strategy was a significant predictor of "integrative generation" ($\beta = .361$, $p < .01$). Model two showed that interpersonal relationship was a significant predictor of a "willingness to change" with an R^2 change of .142 at $p < .01$. The interpersonal relationship with teachers was significant ($\beta = .223$, $p > .01$). However, the interpersonal relationship with students was not statistically significant ($\beta = .097$, $p > .05$).

Based on the results of the blockwise regression analysis, it can be concluded that both instructional strategies, as well as interpersonal relationships, accounted for the variance in the overall transformative learning experience of the students. However, although the perceived influence of the instructional strategies was shown to be a significant predictor of all the four transformative learning subscales, the significance of the students' interpersonal relationship with teachers and with the students varied with the different subscales. The interpersonal relationship with both teachers and students was not a significant predictor for the "awareness of need to change" variable. The interpersonal relationship with students was a significant predictor for the "willingness to change" variable but the interpersonal relationship with teachers was not. The interpersonal relationship with teachers was a significant predictor for both reflective practice and integrative generation but not the students. This could be an indication that the instructional strategies that are used will create the awareness of a need to change. However, in order for the person to take the next step in desiring to change and move on further in the transformative levels of learning experience, interpersonal relationships play significant role. At the level of creating the desire or willingness to change, the students seem to play significant role but then the teachers play a significant role in the subsequent levels. This agrees with Boyd and Myer's conclusion, who say that the learning group as a social system "can provide supportive structures that facilitate an individual's work in realizing personal transformation."[4]

Demographic Information

The instrument sought to determine the occurrence of an extraordinary event that may have happened while the students were studying at the institution.

Table 22. Extraordinary Events Experienced

Response	Frequency N=137	%
Marriage	22	16.06
Birth of a child	23	16.79
Moving to a new place of residence	23	16.79

---

4. Boyd and Myers, "Transformative Education," quoted in Cranton, *Understanding*, 167.

Response	Frequency N=137	%
Divorce/separation	3	2.19
Death of a loved one	36	26.28
Change of job	25	18.25
Loss of a job	8	5.84
Other	10	7.30

There were sixteen students whose mean values for their perceived transformative learning experiences were below 3.0. Among these, three of them reported that they got married, three of them reported that they had a child, five reported having lost a loved one, one person reported a change of a job, three of them reported loss of a job, and three did not report any extraordinary event that happened. Since it is only a few of those who have had an extraordinary experience that had a mean value of less than 3.0, it will be difficult to say at this point that those have been the factors responsible for a reduced transformative learning experience.

Some of the influences mentioned under the "others" category included student responsibilities given in the church, shortage of financial support and the ethnic conflict in different parts of the country.

Table 23. Demographic Information

Response	Frequency	%
Gender		
Male	111	82.8
Female	23	17.2
Marital Status		
Single	63	47.0
Married	69	51.0
Divorced/Separate	1	.70
Widowed	1	.70

Response	Frequency	%
Educational Level Prior to College		
Highschool	33	24.6
Diploma	61	45.5
Bachelors	34	25.4
Associate	2	1.5
Masters	4	2.9
Age		
21–29	50	37.3
30–39	53	39.6
40–49	25	18.7
50–59	6	4.5

N=137

A test for any significant relationship between the demographic information and the perceived transformative learning indicated that there was no statistically significant relationship between the perceived transformative learning experience and the gender ($r = -.104$, $p = .233$) or age ($r = -.038$, $p = .662$) or educational background ($r = .091$, $p = .296$), or marital status ($r = -.054$, $p = .538$).

Gender is not correlated to any of the other demographic data. However, as can be expected, there is a statistically significant correlation between age, education, and marital status. This indicates that the older the student is, the higher would be the possibility of students' level of education and the more likely the person is to be married.

CHAPTER 5

Summary, Conclusion, and Recommendations

This chapter provides a summary of the perception of a transformative learning experience and two of the possible predictive factors for it within the theological higher educational institutions that participated in this study. It includes a summary of the research purpose, research questions, research findings, conclusions, applications, and recommendations.

Research Purpose

The purpose of this mixed method of study was to determine the factors that may explain the students' self-reported transformation, or the lack of it, as a result of their study at the ACTEA-related theological institutions in Ethiopia. The researcher hopes that the determination of such factors within the Ethiopian context will help improve the quality of learning provided within the theological higher educational institutions. As a result, it will improve the quality of graduates that would engage in strengthening the church as it carries out the mission of God. The following were the research questions that this study sought to explore.

Research Questions

1. To what extent do students studying at the ACTEA-related theological colleges in Ethiopia understand themselves to have had a transformative learning experience?

2. To what extent do instructional strategies predict or explain self-reported transformative learning in students studying at the ACTEA-related theological colleges in Ethiopia?

   H_o1: There is no statistically significant relationship between the perceived transformative learning and the instructional strategies used in class and out of class within the ACTEA-related theological institutions in Ethiopia.

3. Is there is a difference between the teachers' and the students' perceptions of the instructional strategies that predict students' transformative learning experience?

   H_o2: There is no statistically significant difference in the perceptions of the students and the teachers on the predictive relationship of the perceived transformative learning and the instructional strategies used in class and out of class within the ACTEA-related theological institutions.

4. To what extent do student interactions with other individuals in the college predict or explain self-reported transformative learning experience in students studying at the ACTEA-related theological colleges in Ethiopia?

   Ho3: There is no statistically significant relationship between the students' perceived transformative learning and their interactions with other individuals within the college.

5. To what extent is the self-reported transformative learning experience of students in full-time study different from those in part-time studies?

   H_o4: There is no statistically significant relationship between the students' perceived transformative learning and their program of study.

Summary of Findings

The summary of the findings for each of the research questions is presented as follows.

Research Question 1

To what extent do students studying at the ACTEA-related theological colleges in Ethiopia understand themselves to have had a transformative learning experience?

The extent students perceived to have experienced transformative learning was measured using nineteen items. The nineteen items formed the four subscales, namely, awareness of the need to change, willingness to change, reflective practice, and integrative generation. Close to all the students (99.3 percent) reported that they had become aware of a need to change as they learned new things and were able to explain things they did not know before. A lesser number of them (95.6 percent) reported that they became willing to change as they were open to listen to new ideas and try out new things. A number of the students (94.2 percent) indicated that they have begun to reflect how they may change, and they have actually tried out new ways of behavior. Finally, 92.7 percent of the students have indicated that they have integrated the new things they have learned into their lives and they are actually able to generate new ideas.

In a separate question, the participants were asked, "do you believe you have experienced a time when you realized that some of your values, beliefs, opinions or way you do things have changed as a result of your studies at the college?" The response shows that 92.2 percent of them confirmed that they have experienced transformation. This figure is very close to the number of participants who reported that they had an integrative generation level of a transformative learning experience (92.7 percent).

A one-way ANOVA showed that there was no statistically significant difference among the five colleges in terms of the transformative learning experiences the students had as a result of their studies at the colleges.

The participants provided examples of areas of transformation they have experienced as a result of their studies at the colleges. The examples were related to (1) beginning to value spiritual practices and others, (2) character, (3) knowledge and understanding, (4) ability to analyze and evaluate, (5) apply to life and ministry, (6) ministerial skills, and (7) social skills. These areas were broadly grouped into three categories namely, deep change (characterization), change in cognitive frame of reference, and skill formation. Close to all the participants who responded to this question reported that they had some change related to their cognitive frame of reference, indicating that they have gained knowledge and understanding that has changed some of their perspectives on the way they did things and the things they held to be true. A lesser number of students (72.2 percent) reported that they have experienced change which has improved their skills. An even lesser number of students (63.3 percent) reported that they have experienced a deep change that has affected their character.

A comparison of the examples from the five institutions showed a greater transformation in areas of cognition and lesser levels of transformation in relation to character and skill. The participants from one of the colleges (C1) indicated that there was a relatively similar number of students that experienced transformation in all three areas.

The focus group discussions also confirmed that students experience transformative learning in relation to their knowledge, but a number of the participants were reluctant to say that most of the students had experienced a change in their character and skill.

The focus groups also gave examples of areas of transformation that students would have experienced. The examples that were given fall into similar categories as the ones that were collected through the survey instrument. These related to cognitive skills, change in attitude and way of seeing things, new skills, character, and social skills.

There were six different factors that were identified by the focus groups as contributors to the perceived transformative learning experiences. These were related to (1) the content of what is taught; (2) the teachers' personality, exemplary life, their approach to students, and the effort they put in teaching; (3) the influence of other students as they study together, discussion times both in class and out of class, exemplary lives of the students, care for each other, and times of fellowship; (4) college-related factors that include college-organized times of prayer and worship, system of accountability that encourages teachers to carry out their responsibilities as well as help students to perform at a higher standard, availability of facilities that are conducive for learning, and relevance of the curriculum; (5) a teaching methodology that is conducive for student learning; and (6) the students' personal effort in their own learning.

Research Question 2

To what extent do instructional strategies predict or explain self-reported transformative learning in students studying at the ACTEA-related theological colleges in Ethiopia?

Null Hypothesis 1

There is no statistically significant relationship between the perceived transformative learning and the instructional strategies used in class and out of class within the ACTEA-related theological institutions in Ethiopia.

There were two questions asked in relation to the instructional strategies that teachers used. The first question (question 7) asked for students to indicate the frequency that each of the instructional strategies was used. The second question (question 8) asked for the students' perception of the influence each instructional strategy had on students' transformative learning experience. A look at the top nine instructional strategies showed that the students' most frequent learning experiences included taking exams, working on some form of assignments, lectures, and question and answers. A lesser frequency was noticed in relation to out-of-classroom practical work and in-class student engagement.

The top two most influential instructional strategies remained the same as those that were listed as being most frequent. The writing of research papers moved higher up, indicating that the students perceived it to be influential. Another interesting observation was that note-taking came higher up. Although the frequency for note taking was less, it was perceived to be an influential practice. On the other hand, one of the instructional strategies that moved further down on the list was group presentation. Although it was one of the three most frequently used instructional strategies, it had a lesser influence on the students' perceived transformative learning experience. Overall, instructional strategies that required the students to be more engaged have moved higher up. Some of these strategies that have moved higher include question and answer, note-taking and small group discussions.

Pearson's correlation for relationship between the students' perceived influence of the instructional strategies and their perceived transformative learning scale was significant t $(136) = .1946$, $r_{IsTl} = .437$, $p < .01$. Pearson's correlation also indicated a significant relationship between the perceived influence of the instructional strategies and the subscales – awareness of need to change (r_{IsAn} = .254, p < .01), willingness to change (r_{IsWc} = .328, p < .01), reflective practice (r_{IsRp} = .412, p < .01) and integrative generation (r_{IsIg} = .400, p < .01).

Linear regression was used to test if the perceived influence of the instructional strategies significantly predicted or explained the perceived transformative learning experience scale. The results of the regression indicated the predictor explained 19.10 percent of the variance (R^2 = .191, F(1,135) = 31.80, p < .001). It was found that the students' perceived influence of instructional strategies significantly explained the perceived transformative learning experience (β = .33, p < .001).

The null hypothesis is therefore rejected indicating that the relationship between the students' perceived transformative learning and the instructional strategies used was statistically significant. This agrees with the findings of both Madsen and King. Jane Vella also supports this in stating that there is more learning in a classroom where a presentation is followed up with materials that catalysis and synthesis, creative work and argument, learners are engaged, in small groups and in large group, in constructing, not just in receiving, content.[1]

Research Question 3

To what extent are there differences in the perceptions of the students and the teachers on the predictive relationship of the instructional strategies and perceived transformative learning experience?

Null Hypothesis 2

There is no statistically significant difference in the perceptions of the students and the teachers on the predictive relationship of the perceived transformative learning and the instructional strategies used within the ACTEA-related theological institutions.

The teachers reported a similar list of instructional strategies as being most frequent as did the students. Of the instructional strategies eight were mentioned by both the teachers and students as being among the top ten most frequent instructional strategies. They differed on the use of group presentations, whole-class discussions, demonstrations, and summary and reflections.

---

1. Vella, *Taking Learning to Task*, 18.

A t-test for independent groups showed that there was no statistically significant difference between the perception of the teachers on the top ten most frequently used instructional strategies (M = 3.98, SD = .10, n = 10) and that of the students (M = 4.04, SD = .10, n=10) at t(18) = 2.10, p = .63 (2 tail). The null hypothesis is not rejected in relation to the teachers' perceived frequency of the instructional strategies and that of the students.

The instructional strategies that the teachers perceived to be most influential were different from the instructional strategies both the teachers and the students reported to be most frequent. The top five influential strategies the teachers reported were demonstration and illustration, question and answer, group class presentation, research papers, and individual class presentation. The lecture method came in sixth place. Instructional strategies that were related to exams were perceived to have less influence on students' transformative learning experience.

A t-test for two independent samples showed that the difference between the perception of the teachers on the top ten most influential instructional strategies (M = 3.42, SD = .04, n = 10) and that of the students (M = 3.62, SD = .03, n=10) was statistically significant, t(18) = 2.10, p < .01 (2-tail). Therefore, the null hypothesis is rejected in relation to the presence of a difference between the teachers' perceived influence of the instructional strategies and that of the students.

It can be observed that while a great number of the students perceived lecture, mid-term and final exams, and summary and reflection very highly, the teachers perceived them to have a lesser influence. The teachers perceive question and answer, small group discussions, whole-class discussions to be more influential to students' transformative learning experience. The results of the focus group discussions provide some clarity on this quantitative result. Four of the most important ones will be briefly shared as follows.

The first one is in relation to the lecture method. The lecture method is reported as the most frequent and most influential instructional strategy by the students. The focus group data does confirm that as well. However, it clarifies that the usefulness of the lecture method is determined by the extent it engages the students in the learning process. This is best done by using the lecture method in combination with other instructional strategies such as small group, question, and answer, whole-class discussion, personal reflection, etc.

The second instructional strategy to consider is group projects and assignments. It is reported by the students as the third most frequent and one of the top ten most influential instructional strategies. However, the focus group data indicates that although the method is valuable, the students believed that its use has not been very fruitful. Instead, it has caused harm to some students who were allowing others to do the work while they themselves were not engaged in the learning. A number of the groups have expressed the opinion that this instructional strategy should not be used, or its use should be reduced. Where it is used, the groups suggested that certain important measures be taken to ensure that all members of the groups are engaged in the work.

The quantitative results indicated that quiz is one of the top ten frequently used instructional strategy, but it has dropped off the list of the top ten most influential instructional strategies both from the perception of the teachers as well as the students. However, the focus group indicated that the students actually would like to see the teachers use quizzes more regularly to help them keep up with their readings of the course material they are learning. On the other hand, they believe final exams encourage memorization for the exam. Two of the colleges believed that final exams do not contribute much to students' transformative learning experience and hence should not be used, or their use should be reduced. It was preferred by one group from one of the colleges because it allowed for objective grading of the work in comparison to a research paper that is graded subjectively.

Finally, note-taking is in the top ten of the most frequent and most influential instructional strategies. The focus group data confirms its important influence on learning, but it also indicates that it is a method that many of the students are not taking advantage of. The reason that was given for this was that the students wait to receive the lecture notes from the teachers, and they use that to prepare for the exams. The focus tends to be more on the preparation for exams rather than learning for transformative learning experience.

The classroom observations showed the frequent use of lectures in combination with limited illustration, question and answer, use of the black/whiteboard, and students taking notes. The level of engagement through pair and share or whole-class discussion happened in less than 50 percent of the classes that were observed. In a couple of classes, teachers asked questions, but students were not responding. It was observed that in two of the classes, student engagement was affected by the degree of students' language competency and clarity of the subject matter.

Research Question 4

To what extent do student interactions with other individuals in the college predict or explain self-reported transformative learning experience in students studying at the ACTEA-related theological colleges in Ethiopia?

Null Hypothesis 3

There is no statistically significant relationship between the students' perceived transformative learning and their interactions with other individuals within the college.

The mean values for the influences the teachers, students, and administrative staff had on the students were all above 3.0. This was an indication of agreement to the presence of influence on the students' perceived transformative learning experience. There were some students (7.3 percent) who did not perceive to have been influenced by the teachers or the students or the administrative staff in any way.

It is worth noting that the mean values for the influences of the students, as well as the teachers, were very close to each other. The mean values of the teachers' influence out of class and the influence of the administrative staff were rated lowest.

A t-test for two independent samples was done to test for difference between the students' perception of the influence of the interpersonal relationships on their perceived transformative learning experience (M = 3.27, SD = 0.07, n = 7) to that of the teachers' (M = 3.31, SD = 0.05, n = 7). The difference was not statistically significant t(12) = 2.18, p = .67 (2-tail).

A blockwise multiple regression analysis indicated that the two independent variables – interpersonal relationships with teachers and administrative staff and interpersonal relationships with the students – explained 28.20 percent of the variance ($R2 = .282$, $F(2,134) = 26.3$, at $p < 0.01$). It was found that interpersonal relationships with teachers and administrative staff significantly explained transformative learning experience ($\beta = .186$, $p < .01$) as did interpersonal relationships with other students ($\beta = .145$, $p < .01$).

Therefore, the null hypothesis is rejected, and it can be concluded that there is a statistically significant relationship between the students' perceived transformative learning and their interactions with other individuals within the college.

The participants in the study identified different examples of how they have been influenced by the teachers, the students, and the administrative staff. A largest percent was related to the influence of the teachers. Four categories of teacher influences were mentioned.

The first one is the teacher's influence in class, which happens as the teachers take time to recognize student differences and are able to engage them in class. They were done as the teachers took the time to know the students by name and provide help as they needed help. The second one is the effort the teachers put into the students' learning. The teachers who recognize that they were investing in students who reach into places where they themselves would not be able to, would have a greater influence on the students.

The third category is the teachers' out-of-class interaction with students. Some of the teachers who visited students at home when they were sick or were taking time to be with the students – having tea, sharing their lives with them, and praying for them, have been influential. While they affirmed the influence some of the teachers had on students outside of the class, almost all the groups have mentioned that teachers are mostly not with students outside of class. Finally, teachers' exemplary life was also reported as being influential. One demonstration of this was their attendance in chapel with students, but it also included the way they lived their lives, which the students observed.

Although it was to a lesser extent, the students were also reported to have had an influence on the perceived transformative learning experiences they had. There were three categories that showed the different ways students influenced others. The first category was in-class interaction with students through small group discussions and group work assignments which gave them opportunities to learn from each other. The classroom observation has also shown that there was a good combination of lectures and student-engaging instructional strategies. It has also shown that there was a higher level of interpersonal relationships occurring among the students and with the teachers. The second category was related to the out-of-class interactions students had. The times they had in worship, service, and care for others, provided growing experiences for them. Finally, the exemplary lives of some of the students were also mentioned as being influential.

Research Question 5

To what extent is the self-reported transformative learning experience of students in full-time study different from those in part-time studies?

Null Hypothesis 4

There is no statistically significant difference between students in part-time studies and those in full-time studies in their perceived transformative learning experience.

Close to 80 percent of the students indicated that they were enrolled as full-time students and the remaining 20 percent were enrolled as part-time students. The perceived students' transformative learning experience between students in the part-time study and those in the full-time study were not significantly correlated, $r = .074$, $p < .05$. A t-test for two independent samples tested for a significant difference in the perceived transformative learning experience between the students in their part-time studies (M = 3.65, SD = .28) and those in full-time studies (M = 3.58, SD = .38). The difference was not statistically significant, $t(132) = 1.96$, $p = .596$. Therefore, the null hypothesis was not rejected.

Three-Factor Multiple Regression

A three-factor multiple regression was tested to determine the extent of instructional strategies and interpersonal relationships (teacher and administrative staff and other students) predicted or explained the perceived transformative learning. The result of the multiple regression indicated that the three independent variables explained 31.8 percent of the variance ($R2 = .318$, $F(3,133) = 20.6$, at $p < 0.01$). It was found that the interpersonal relationship with teacher and administrative staff significantly predicted transformative learning experience ($\beta = .286$, $p < .005$) as did the perceived influence of instruction strategies ($\beta = .223$, $p < .005$) and other students ($\beta = .183$, $p < .005$). The extent the three IVs explained the perceived transformative learning is only just over 30 percent, which indicates that there are other factors that would explain the remaining 70 percent of the perceived transformative learning experience the students had.

Demographic data

A test for any significant relationship between the demographic information and the perceived transformative learning indicated that there was no statistically significant relationship between the perceived transformative learning experience and gender ($r = -.104$, $p = .233$), or age ($r = -.038$, $p = .662$), or educational background ($r = .091$, $p = .296$), or marital status ($r = -.054$, $p = .538$).

Gender is not correlated to any of the other demographic data. However, there is a statistically significant correlation between age, education, and marital status. This indicates that the older the student is, the more likely it is that the student would have a higher level of education and the more likely it is that person would be married.

Relation to the Theoretical Framework

The theoretical framework was a transformative learning process that moved through five stages – namely, learning experiences, reflection with appreciation, speculation and goal setting, practice of new roles, and integration. These five stages were collapsed into three constructs by combining learning experiences and reflection with speculation to be awareness of a need to change, speculation and goal setting and practice of new roles to be reflective practice, and finally the integrative generation. The exploratory factor analysis resulted in four constructs by splitting the first construct into two and keeping the other two constructs as they were.

The study has shown that students progressed through these four stages with 99.3 percent at the awareness of need, 95.6 percent at the willingness to change, 94.2 percent at the reflective practice and 92.7 percent at the integrative generation stage as shown in figure 12.

Conclusions

The purpose of this study was to determine possible predictive factors that contributed to the student's perceived transformative learning experiences while studying at the ACTEA-related theological colleges in Ethiopia. The study involved the collection of quantitative data as well as qualitative data through focus group discussions and classroom observation. The data were

Summary, Conclusion, and Recommendations

Conclusion One

Almost all the students (99.3 percent) reported that they had become aware of a need to change as they learned new things and became able to explain things they did not know before. A lesser number of them (95.6 percent) reported that they became willing to change as they were open to listen to new ideas and try out new things. A number of the students (94.2 percent) indicated that they have begun to reflect on how they may change, and they have actually tried out new ways of behavior. Finally, 92.7 percent of the students indicated that they have integrated the new things they have learned into their lives and they were actually able to generate new ideas.

Therefore, it can be concluded that almost all the students have changed in the knowledge they had and their ability to explain things they did not know before and over 90 percent of the students reported that they have experienced a higher level of transformation in some areas as they were able to integrate what they learned to their lives and ministry. Figure 13 shows the number of students who reported transformation at the different levels of the transformative learning process.

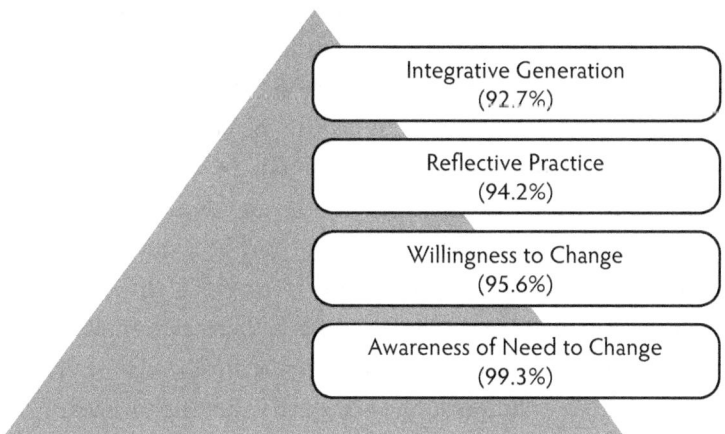

Figure 13: Transformative learning pyramid

As can be seen in figure 13, the gap between those who became aware of a need to change and those at the integrative generation level is very small (7 percent) indicating that most of the students at the colleges have perceived a growing transformative learning experience due to their studies at the colleges.

The one-way ANOVA test has shown that there is no statistically significant difference among the colleges in terms of the extent the students from these colleges perceived to have experienced transformative learning.

The areas of transformation included deep change (character), change in cognitive frame of reference, and skill formation. This is also in agreement with what Taylor says regarding the holistic nature of transformative learning. He states that research substantiates the importance of a holistic approach to learning that recognizes the role of feelings and relationships with others in addition to the often-emphasized use of rational discourse in the process of transformative learning.[2]

Almost all the students experienced some change in relation to the cognitive frame of reference, indicating they have gained knowledge and understanding that has changed some of their perspectives on the way they did things and the things they held to be true. A lesser number of students (72.2 percent) gave examples related to change in skills and an even lesser number of students gave examples related to change in character (63.3 percent). Although this gives a general picture of the extent students experience transformation in the different areas, it may not be sufficient to conclude that students' perceived transformation had to do more with the cognition and much less with skill and character. It may not be possible to make this conclusion because the participants were only giving examples of changes they experienced. In doing that, they may have given more of cognitive changes and less of the others considering the time they had to write their experiences and the limited space given on the instrument. However, the focus group discussion has given an indication that there were students who did not experience much of a transformation in the areas of character and skill.

The possible contributors to the perceived transformative learning were related to (1) content of what is taught; (2) teachers' personality, exemplary life, their approach to students, and the effort they put in teaching; (3) other

---

2. Taylor, "Transformative Learning Theory," 11.

students' influence as they study together, discussion times both in class and out of class, exemplary lives of the students, care for each other, and times of fellowship; (4) college-related factors – which include college-organized times of prayer and worship, system of accountability that encourages teachers to carry out their responsibilities as well as help students to perform at a higher standard, availability of facilities that are conducive for learning, and relevance of the curriculum; (5) teaching methodology that is conducive for student learning; and (6) students' personal effort in their own learning.

Conclusion Two

The result of linear regression analysis has shown that the students' perceived influence of instructional strategies, significantly explained the perceived transformative learning experience (β = .437, p < .001) accounting for 19.1 percent of the variance. This is also in line with Madsen and Cook's study where the learning activities and assignments predicted two of the transformative learning subscales (awareness of need to change and prediction of future behavior).[3] It is also supported by King's findings that showed that 68.6 percent of the participants indicated that learning activities and assignments contributed to the perceived transformative learning.[4]

A t-test for two independent samples showed that the difference between the perception of the teachers on the top ten most influential instructional strategies (M = 3.42, SD = .04, n = 10) and that of the students (M = 3.62, SD = .03, n=10) was statistically significant, t(18) = 2.10, p = .00 (2-tail).

While there is a statistically significant difference between the teachers and the students understanding of the extent the instructional strategies were influential, the focus group clarified that they both believed instructional strategies that actively engaged students in their learning were influential. As a result, lectures (one of the mass instructional strategies) was perceived to be one of the most influential instructional strategies. However, its influence is determined by the degree it engaged the students in the learning process. With the intent of making the learning process more engaging, both students as well as teachers included instructional strategies such as question and answer, small group discussion, and presentation (group instructional

---

3. Madsen and Cook, "Transformative Learning."
4. King, "Examining Learning Activities."

strategies) as part of the top ten most influential instructional strategies. The other instructional strategies that were included in the top ten most influential strategies were quizzes, note-taking, and writing research papers (individualized instructional strategies).

The perception that the lecture method continues to be an influential tool is in line with what Mekonnen says regarding the lecture method. He explains, "Despite an overabundance of other teaching methods being available, the face-to-face expository talk or 'lecture' still holds a central position at many levels of education and will undoubtedly continue to do so for some considerable time to come."[5] While the value of lectures to education remains true, the students seem to perceive lectures, which are a mass instructional strategy, to be influential when it is used in combination with other instructional strategies that engage the students in class through individual instructional strategies (quiz, research papers, individual class presentations) and group instructional strategies (small group discussions, whole-class discussions, and case studies).

Barth is quoted in Shaw confirming the need for a combination of instructional strategies and not the lecture method alone in teaching. He says,

> Lecturing is an unnatural act, an act for which Providence did not design humans. It is perfectly all right now and then to speak while others remain silent, but to do so regularly, one hour at a time, for one person to drone on and on while others sit in silence, I do not believe that this is what the Creator designed humans to do.[6]

As it is illustrated in figure 14, an influential instructional process should have the students engaged individually, in groups, and as a whole class. The interaction of all these together is perceived to lead to a more influential learning process.

---

5. Mekonnen, *General Learning-Teaching Methods*, 114.
6. Barth, *Learning by Heart*, 34–35, quoted in Shaw, *Transforming Theological Education*, 183.

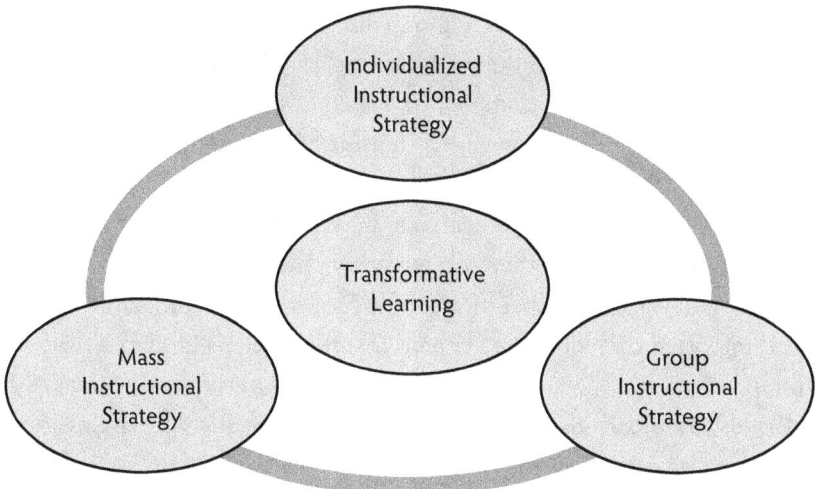

Figure 14: Interactive instructional strategies for transformative learning

Conclusion Three

A blockwise multiple regression analysis has shown that interpersonal relationships with teachers and administrative staff significantly explained transformative learning experience ($\beta = .186$, $p < .01$) as did the interpersonal relationship with other students ($\beta = .145$, $p < .01$), accounting for 28.2 percent of the variance. King's study also shows that 70 percent of the time the students perceived their transformative learning was influenced by a relationship with other people.[7] This is also in agreement with Wubbel who postulates that the amount of cooperation a teacher exhibits has an influence on the students. He explains cooperation as that which involves demonstrating concern for each student and building a sense of community within the classroom. It is established first and foremost in the way students interpret the actions of the teacher as evidence for or against the teacher's desire for cooperation.[8]

Both the teachers and students were reported as being influential to a similar extent. However, the influence of the teachers outside of class and that of the administrative staff was rated low. This indicates that the opportunities to access the teachers outside of class are limited, a finding that

---

7. King, *Handbook of the Evolving Research*, Kindle Locations, 1136–1141.
8. Wubbels, "Interpersonal Relationships," 151–70, quoted in Marzano, *Art and Science of Teaching*, 152.

was supported through the focus group discussion. The administrative staff may not have much interaction with students at all due to the nature of their responsibilities or they are not easily accessible.

In spite of the reported low levels outside of classroom interactions, the students reported that their interactions with teachers outside of class and their exemplary lives were influential to the students' perceived transformative learning experience. They also report that the in-class interactions with teachers and teachers' preparation for the class have been influential. This is also supported by Wubbel's statement that the teachers influence students through dominance, which he explains as clarity of purpose and guidance. It provides both clear academic direction and requires adherence to classroom rules and procedures.[9] Besides the influence of the teachers, the students also perceived that the interpersonal relationships they had with other students within the classrooms, outside of classrooms, and the exemplary lives of the students as influential to their transformative learning experience.

Conclusion Four

Interpersonal relationships were found to be significant predictors of the students' perceived transformative learning experiences. While the instructional strategies continue to be significant predictors of all the four constructs, the interpersonal relationships are significant predictors of three of the constructs (willingness to change, reflective practice, and integrative generation). While the interpersonal relationships with students explained more of the "willingness to change" construct, the interpersonal relationships with teachers and administrative staff significantly explained the "reflective practice" and "integrative generation" constructs.

Conclusion Five

There was no statistically significant correlation between students' transformative learning experience and their program of study (part-time or full-time) ($r = .074$, $p < .05$). A t-test for two independent samples also indicated that there was no statistically significant difference between students in their part-time studies ($M = 3.65$, $SD = .28$) and those in full-time studies ($M =$

---

9. Wubbels, "Interpersonal Relationships," quoted in Marzano, *Art and Science of Teaching*, 150.

3.58, SD = .38). The difference was not statistically significant, t(132) = 1.96, p = .596. Therefore, the null hypothesis was not rejected, showing that there is no difference in the degree of perceived transformative learning between students in part-time and full-time study. However, a student from C1 has said that they envy students who are studying on a full-time basis as it gives them time to read a lot and take time in doing the assignments. Even though there is no statistical difference in the perception of the transformative learning experience, there may be a difference in the extent of transformative learning experience they had, which is not explored in this study.

Applications

The study sought to determine the extent that transformative learning has occurred among the graduating students from five of the evangelical theological higher educational institutions. It also sought to determine the factors that may explain the perceived transformative learning experiences that students reported. The following are some of the applications that can be drawn from the findings of this study.

Application One

The mission of theological education is to strengthen the mission of the church as it trains men and women who are capable of guiding and empowering the church to be effective in fulfilling its mission.[10] The extent the graduates from the theological educational institutions can contribute to the transformative ministry of the church and its impact in the world is determined by the extent the graduates themselves are holistically transformed in their cognitive, affective, and behavioral domains. Therefore, it is important for theological higher educational institutions that the students not only complete their studies, but they come out holistically transformed and equipped to strengthen the church. In order to do this, it may be necessary that colleges have a strict screening procedure for a clear purpose in joining the college. It is tempting for institutions to attract as many students as possible in order to sustain theological education financially. That is likely to affect the degree

---

10. Shaw, *Transforming Theological Education*; Ferris, Lillis, and Enlow, *Ministry Education*.

of transformation the graduates would experience. Therefore, institutions may need to clearly decide on their purpose and recruit students accordingly.

Application Two

It is possible to become content with the students knowing facts and doing well on exams and graduating. There may need to be an increased discontentment in the teachers and administrative staff to strive until the students begin to move up the ladder in the transformative learning process causing them to desire to change, trying out the different ways to change, and integrating what they have learned into their lives and ministry. The transmission of information to the students, and helping them understand what it is, is not enough. They need to be able to see its relevance for them. This is in line with what Coley says, "learning is more likely to take place when people see the relevance of what is taught . . . Given that Jesus's teaching took place in response to the real situations he faced, the disciples could immediately recognize its relevance."[11] It is only when students are captured by the relevance of what they are learning that they would be able to try it out and integrate it into their life, which is the ultimate purpose in teaching. Teachers and administrative staff should strive to this end.

Application Three

Teachers perceived instructional strategies that actively engage students in their learning are more influential in students' transformative learning. However, the instructional strategies they used most frequently, were different from what they believed to be influential. Therefore, it is clear that the teachers know that engaging the students in learning is most influential. However, it appears that since lecturing seems to be an easier method to use in teaching, requiring nothing more than gathering information to transmit to the students, teachers end up lecturing with minimum amount of student engagement. As one of the participants said, the students are capable of reaching into places where the teachers would not dream of being. Therefore, the effort the teachers put in to equipping the students will be their way of reaching into those places through the students. This requires a willingness to

---

11. Coley, "How Would it Play," 428.

invest oneself in the organization of instruction that actively engages students in the learning process.

Application Four

The students come from different backgrounds. Their educational backgrounds, language competencies, and preferred way of learning are all different. Therefore, it is not possible to think that "one-size-fits-all." Teachers, as part of their act of being invested in the teaching of the students, need to recognize the difference among the students and organize their learning accordingly. Differentiation happens in relation to the content they are learning, the process of learning, and the way students are required to demonstrate their learning. Among the many examples that were mentioned of the differences of the students, one of them was related to the fact that some students prefer being assessed through final exams while others would rather be assessed through writing research papers. Therefore, the teacher may consider creating diversity in the assessment process.

This idea of differentiation is also supported by Dosch and Zidon who say that there is a "mismatch between college instruction and students" academic needs. In addition, the current educational system works hard to keep the traditional ideals and "one-size-fits-all" methods in place rather than employing more learner-centered approaches.[12] Tomlinson and Allan also explain the diversity of the learners and the need to diversify the instructional strategies used in the classrooms.

> A teacher who is comfortable and skilled with the use of multiple instructional strategies is more likely to reach out effectively to varied students than is the teacher who uses a single approach to teaching and learning. Teachers are particularly limited when the sole or primary instructional strategy is teacher-centered (such as lecture), or drill-and-practice (such as worksheets).[13]

---

12. Dosch and Zidon, "Course Fits Us," 343.
13. Tomlinson and Allan, *Leadership for Differentiating*, 11.

Application Five

In the use of instructional strategies, students would like to see a combination of different instructional strategies being used in teaching. They would like to have a lecture that is combined with instructional strategies that engage the students in their learning such as group discussions, class discussions, case studies, etc. They would also like to have instructional strategies that get them engaged on their own, such as personal reflection, research papers, quizzes, and individual presentations. This is also similar to King's finding in which readings and class discussions were rated highest.[14]

They would like to see less of the group project works and group presentations since they are not giving all the students the opportunity to grow through them. The students recognize their value in working together and learning from each other, but their experience is that many students have the tendency to leave the work for a few students to do. Teachers who desire to continue with this method, especially those who have big classes, may need to consider how they may hold each student accountable to the work. Davis also recognizes this challenge with regard to group works and gives helpful strategies for dealing with uncooperative group members.[15] Final exams are also perceived to be less influential in contributing students' transformative learning experience since they place great emphasis on memorization.

Application Six

The students reported that teachers are significantly influential in the students' perceived transformative learning. The teachers are perceived to be men and women with a lot of life and ministry experience. The students voiced their desire to learn from the experiences and lives of the teachers. They seek a relationship with the teachers which they feel they are not getting from most of the teachers. As one of the students from C5 said,

> You would want the teachers to come and encourage you, but what you see is the teachers teach and just leave. What I would want is to have the teachers have tea with me during the break time. They don't even eat lunch together. So where is the

---

14. King, *Handbook of Evolving Research*, Kindle Locations 1175–1176.
15. Davis, *Tools for Teaching*, 190–97.

relationship coming from? If we ate together and had time to talk, I believe the relationship would build.

Teachers will be able to personally influence the students in their personal relationships outside of class. As the students are asking for this to happen, teachers may want to consider how they may be able to do that with students beyond the classroom interactions.

Application Seven

The students' perceived transformative learning experience is also influenced by their interaction with one another. The opportunities some of the institutions created for student interactions – such as ministering together, time of worship together, working together in groups, and visiting those who are in need – have all contributed towards the students' perceived transformative learning experience. This becomes an encouragement for institutions to continue providing such opportunities that allow for student interaction both within the classroom as well as outside of the classroom.

This is also supported by the quantitative analysis that has shown that the students have a significant influence on other students' desiring to change. Cranton also supports this and suggests creating supportive groups using small group activities or discussions during which learners can get to know each other and develop a relationship, placing students into project groups for them to work together, encouraging study partnerships or groups, and using peer teaching where participants share expertise with each other, etc.[16]

For Further Study

Since the knowledge base on the area of transformative learning within the Ethiopian evangelical theological higher education is limited, further study in this area will help in developing leaders who are truly trained to strengthen the church of Ethiopia. Some of the possible recommendations for further study include the following.

---

16. Cranton, *Understanding*, 167.

Recommendation One

Since this is the first study in the area of transformative learning with the Ethiopian evangelical theological higher education, replication of this study will help refine the instrument for the context.

Recommendation Two

The interpersonal relationships and the instructional strategies were able to explain only 32 percent of the perceived transformative learning. A similar study will be good to run in order to determine what other factors contribute to students' perceived transformative learning within the evangelical theological higher educational institutions to account for the remaining 68 percent.

Recommendation Three

This study assumed that all the colleges embraced the idea that they existed to train leaders for the church as stated by Shaw, where the output (graduates who have experienced transformation as a result of their studies), would, in turn, lead to positive outcomes (churches that are more faithful and effective in their missional calling).[17] However, it may be beneficial to study the specific purpose each of the institutions has and assess the extent the graduates are in line with that purpose.

Recommendation Four

The teachers' perception of the influential instructional strategies was very much different from what they frequently used. It will be good to research how to best help the teachers to close down the gap between what is believed to be influential and what is practiced in reality. It may be necessary to assess the extent teachers are comfortably familiar in using diverse instructional strategies that would sufficiently engage students in the instructional process.

Recommendation Five

This study focused on students who are enrolled in the regular program. Since many of the colleges have non-regular programs such as vacation programs, distance education, and online programs, it will be good to see how

---

17. Shaw, "Holistic and Transformative," 209.

the perception of transformative learning would be different or similar in those programs.

Recommendation Six

It was only 67 percent of the participants who gave examples of changes they experienced as a result of their studies at the college and the factors that may have contributed to it. A better result may be obtained if the findings from the focus group discussions on the areas of transformation and the possible contributors to transformative learning are listed in the survey instrument and participants are asked to mark the ones appropriate to their experience.

Chapter Summary

The study sought to determine whether students perceived themselves to have experienced transformative learning and the factors they perceived that may predict or explain transformative learning. The findings have shown that the students did experience transformative learning to a varying degree beginning with an awareness of a need to change and moving up to the stage where they were able to integrate what they have learned with life and ministry. The instructional strategies and interpersonal relationships with teachers and administrative staff and other students were found to be significant predictors of transformative learning. While the instructional strategies predicted all four constructs, the interpersonal relationship explained the willingness to change, reflective practice, and integrative generation, which indicated the significant role relationships with teachers and students have in moving students to demonstrate what they learned in their lives.

Therefore, for a theological institution to produce men and women who are holistically transformed, the institutions need to carefully screen the students they are receiving and the teachers they are inviting to teach. The teachers should also be discontented until they see that their students have a transformative learning experience. They would be able to do this as they put their effort into their preparation for teaching, differentiate their instructions, and create an environment conducive for student transformative learning.

APPENDIX A

Survey Instrument – Students

Agreement to Participate

The research in which you are about to participate in is designed to determine the extent you believe your study at the college has brought change in your life and the factors that may have contributed to it. This research is being conducted by Alemseged Ketema Alemu for purposes of dissertation research.

In this research, you will respond to questions related to how your studies at the college might have changed the way you think, the new skills you may have developed and, and how it may have shaped your character. You will also answer questions that seek to find out the different factors that may have been influential in causing the change in your life.

Any information you provide will be held strictly confidential and at no time will your name be reported, or your name identified with your responses. *Participation in this study is totally voluntary and you are free to withdraw from the study at any time.* By your completion of this survey and checking the appropriate box below, you are giving informed consent for the use of your responses in this research.

☐ I agree to participate
☐ I do not agree to participate

1. Below is a list of statements dealing with your general feelings about your educational experience at this college. Please indicate how strongly you agree or disagree with each statement by placing an "X" in the box that accurately describes your experience.

No	Perceived Changes	Strongly Agree	Agree	Disagree	Strongly Disagree
1.1	I have learned new things I did not know prior to coming to the college.				
1.2	I was able to explain concepts I did not know before or was unsure of.				
1.3	I became open to listening to ideas I did not agree with in the past.				
1.4	I became open to engaging in conversations on topics I used to not agree with.				
1.5	There were occasions when I had developed the desire to act and do things differently.				
1.6	There were occasions when I decided to change or revise some of my beliefs or the way I did somethings.				
1.7	I have considered ways I may start to act differently from my usual beliefs and way of doing things.				
1.8	I have tried to figure out how I may adopt these new ways of acting to my life and ministry.				
1.9	I gathered the information I needed to adopt these new ways of acting.				
1.10	I tried to practice some of the new things I learned so that I would become more comfortable or confident in doing them.				
1.11	I started to act and do somethings differently from the way I used to.				

1.12	I have grown in my ability to solve problems in my personal life and ministry.			
1.13	I am better equipped to judge the values of certain ideas and practices.			
1.14	My studies at the college have changed some of my point of views on certain issues and practices.			
1.15	I now behave differently in some ways because of the change I had in my point of views.			
1.16	I was able to come up with new ways of doing things.			
1.17	Because I have started doing somethings differently, I see change in my life and ministry.			
1.18	I was able to generate ideas that enabled me to do things better.			
1.19	There are somethings I have learned to do without hesitation			

2. Do you believe you have experienced a time when you realized that some of your values, beliefs, opinions or way you do things had changed as a result of your studies at the college?

☐ Yes, if "Yes" please go to question #3 and continue the survey.
☐ No, if "No" please go to question #9 to continue the survey.

3. Briefly describe some of the changes that happened as a result of your studies at the college.

4. Below is a list of statements dealing with your general attitude about the influence the following individuals had in the change you experienced at the college. Please indicate how strongly you agree or disagree with each statement by placing an "X" in the box that accurately describes your experience.

No	Relational Factors	Strongly Agree	Agree	Disagree	Strongly Disagree
4.1	The effort some of the teachers put to have a close relationship with students inside the classroom influenced the change I experienced.				
4.2	The effort some of the teachers to have a close relationship with students outside of the classroom influenced the change I experienced.				
4.3	The effort some of the teachers put to see the students learn influenced some of the changes I experienced.				
4.4	The modeling of some of the teachers influenced some of the changes I experienced.				
4.5	I had opportunities to interact with students in the class that had an influence on some of the change I had experienced.				
4.6	I had opportunities to interact with students out of class that had an influence on some of the change I experienced.				
4.7	The manner of some of the college administrators (principal, academic dean, dean of students, etc) approached the students had an influence on some of the change I experienced.				

Survey Instrument – Students

5. Were there teachers, or students, or administrators who had an influence on the change you experienced while you were studying at the college?

☐ Yes, if "Yes" please go to question #6 and continue the survey.
☐ No, if "No" please go to question #7 to continue the survey.

6. Briefly describe what they did to have that influence on you.

7. Below is a list of learning activities. Please indicate how frequently you think your instructors used each activity at the college by placing an "X" in the appropriate box.

No.	Instructional Strategies	Very Frequently	Frequently	Sometimes	Rarely	Never
7.1	Question and answer					
7.2	Classroom lecture					
7.3	Demonstrations/ illustrations					
7.4	Group Projects/assignments					
7.5	Research papers					
7.6	Assigned reading assignments					
7.7	Individual student class presentations					
7.8	Case studies in class					
7.9	Small group discussions in class					
7.10	Personal reflection					
7.11	Quiz on reading and lectures					
7.12	Mid and final examinations					
7.13	Field trip					
7.14	Homework/practice					
7.15	Note-taking					
7.16	Whole-class discussion					
7.17	Group class presentation					
7.18	Summary/reflection assignments					
7.19	Practicum/internship					

8. Below is a list of in-class and out-of-class learning activities. Please indicate to what extent each activity was influential in your transformative learning experience at the college by placing an "X" in the box that accurately describes your experience.

No	Instructional Strategies	Very Influential	Somewhat influential	Slightly Influential	Not at all Influential
8.1	Question and answer				
8.2	Classroom lecture				
8.3	Demonstrations/ illustrations				
8.4	Group Projects/assignments				
8.5	Research papers				
8.6	Assigned reading assignments				
8.7	Individual student class presentations				
8.8	Case studies in class				
8.9	Small group discussions in class				
8.10	Personal reflection				
8.11	Quiz on reading and lectures				
8.12	Mid and final examinations				
8.13	Field trip				
8.14	Homework/practice				
8.15	Note-taking				
8.16	Whole-class discussion				
8.17	Group class presentation				
8.18	Summary/reflection assignments				
8.19	Practicum/internship				

If there were other learning activities that were influential, please name them below.

9. Which of the following major changes has occurred while you have been attending this college?
    - ☐ Marriage
    - ☐ Birth of child
    - ☐ Moving to new place of residence
    - ☐ Divorce/separation
    - ☐ Death of a loved one
    - ☐ Change of job
    - ☐ Loss of job
    - ☐ Other: _____

10. Which of the following best describes your enrollment at the college?
    - ☐ Studying as a Regular Full-time student
    - ☐ Studying as a part-time student while having full-time employment or enrollment at a different college
    - ☐ Studying as a part-time student while having part-time employment or enrollment at a different college
    - ☐ Studying as a full-time student while having part-time employment or enrollment at a different college

11. Sex:
    - ☐ Male
    - ☐ Female

12. Marital status:
    - ☐ Single
    - ☐ Divorced/Separated
    - ☐ Married
    - ☐ Widowed

13. Prior education:
    - ☐ High school completion certificate
    - ☐ Bachelor's degree
    - ☐ Associates degree
    - ☐ Other: _____
    - ☐ 10+2/10+3 diploma
    - ☐ Master's degree
    - ☐ Doctorate

14. How many semesters have you been enrolled at this college? _____

15. Age:
    - ☐ Below 21
    - ☐ 36–39
    - ☐ 30–35
    - ☐ >60
    - ☐ 50 – 59
    - ☐ 25 – 29
    - ☐ 21–24
    - ☐ 40–49

Thank you for completing this questionnaire.

The instrument is revised with permission from the original Learning Activities Survey developed by Dr. Kathleen King.

APPENDIX B

Focus Group Discussion Questions

Agreement to Participate

The research in which you are about to participate in is designed to determine the extent you believe your study at the college has brought change in your life and the factors that may have contributed to it. This research is being conducted by Alemseged Ketema Alemu for purposes of dissertation research.

In this research, you will respond to questions that will further elaborate on what you have already completed in the survey. related to how your studies at the college might have changed the way you think, the new skills you may have developed and, and how it may have shaped your character. You will also answer questions that seek to find out the different factors that may have been influential in causing the change in your life.

Any information you provide will be held strictly confidential and at no time will your name be reported, or your name identified with your responses. *Participation in this study is totally voluntary and you are free to withdraw from the study at any time.* By your completion of this survey and checking the appropriate box below, you are giving informed consent for the use of your responses in this research.

Name _____

☐ I agree to participate
☐ I do not agree to participate

☐ Full-time
☐ Part-time

1. Do you think students at the college generally experience some level of transformation? What would be some of the areas they experience transformation?
2. What do you think may have contributed to the transformation students experienced or the lack of it at the college?
3. What do you think are the instructional strategies that are most commonly used which are helpful and need to continue being used? What are the instructional strategies that are being used a lot which need to not be used at all? What are the instructional strategies that are not being used much but must be used?
4. On a scale of 1–10, how would you rate the teacher-student relationship at ETC? How would you characterize the most relational person?
5. What do you think should happen in order for the teachers to influence the students' transformation? In class as well as out of class?
6. Do you think you have been influenced in some way by other students at ETC? What do you think should happen to encourage the student-to-student relationships for mutual growth?
7. How has the fact that you are a part-time student affected the extent you experienced transformation at ETC? Some of you have given up a full-time job to be a full-time student. Do you think you have experienced the transformation you hoped for as opposed to studying as a part-time student?

APPENDIX C

Survey Instrument – Teachers

Agreement to Participate

The research in which you are about to participate in is designed to determine the extent you believe your study at the college has brought change in your life and the factors that may have contributed to it. This research is being conducted by Alemseged Ketema Alemu for purposes of dissertation research.

In this research, you will respond to a question on your perception of change students may have experienced as a result of their studies at the college. You will also respond to some questions related to the learning activities you use in your teaching at the college and how frequently you use them.

Any information you provide will be held strictly confidential and at no time will your name be reported, or your name identified with your responses. *Participation in this study is totally voluntary and you are free to withdraw from the study at any time.* By your completion of this survey and checking the appropriate box below, you are giving informed consent for the use of your responses in this research.

☐ I agree to participate
☐ I do not agree to participate

1. Do you believe that students have experienced a time when some of their values, beliefs, opinions or ways they do things changed as a result of their studies at the college?

☐ Yes, if "Yes" please go to question #2 and continue the survey.
☐ No, if "No" please go to question #3 to continue the survey.

2. Please give some examples to show that students who are in their graduating year at the college, have experienced some change as a result of their study?

3. Below is a list of statements dealing with your general opinion about the influence students and academic staff had in the change students experienced at the college. Please indicate how strongly you agree or disagree with each statement by placing an "X" in the box that accurately describes students' experience.

No	Relational Factors	Strongly Agree	Agree	Disagree	Strongly Disagree
2.1	The effort some of the teachers put to have a close relationship with students inside the classroom influenced some of the change students experienced.				
2.2	The effort some of the teachers put to have a close relationship with students outside of the classroom influenced some of the change students experienced.				
2.3	The effort some teachers put to see the students learn influenced some of the change students experienced.				
2.4	The modeling of some of the teachers influenced the change students experienced.				
2.5	Students had opportunities to interact with other students in the classroom that had an influence on the change they experienced.				
2.6	Students had opportunities to interact with other students outside of the classroom that had an influence on the change they experienced.				
2.7	College administrators such as Principal, Academic Dean, Student Dean, etc. influenced some of the change students experienced.				

Survey Instrument – Teachers

4. Below is a list of in-class and out-of-class activities. Please indicate how frequently you believe you have used each activity at the college by placing an "X" in the appropriate box.

No.	Instructional Strategies	Very Frequently	Frequently	Sometimes	Rarely	Never
3.1	Question and answer					
3.2	Classroom lecture					
3.3	Demonstrations/ illustrations					
3.4	Group projects/assignments					
3.5	Research papers					
3.6	Assigned reading assignments					
3.7	Individual student class presentations					
3.8	Case studies in class					
3.9	Small group discussions in class					
3.10	Personal reflection					
3.11	Quiz on reading and lectures					
3.12	Mid and final examinations					
3.13	Field trip					
3.14	Homework/practice					
3.15	Note-taking					
3.16	Whole-class discussion					
3.17	Group class presentation					
3.18	Summary/reflection assignments					
3.19	Practicum/internship					

5. Below is a list of in-class and out-of-class learning activities. Please indicate to what extent you believe each activity was influential in students' transformative learning experience at the college by placing an "X" in the box that accurately describes your opinion.

No	Instructional Strategies	Very Influential	Somewhat influential	Slightly Influential	Not at all Influential
4.1	Question and answer				
4.2	Classroom lecture				
4.3	Demonstrations/ illustrations				
4.4	Group projects/assignments				
4.5	Research papers				
4.6	Assigned reading assignments				
4.7	Individual student class presentations				
4.8	Case studies in class				
4.9	Small group discussions in class				
4.10	Personal reflection				
4.11	Quiz on reading and lectures				
4.12	Mid and final examinations				
4.13	Field trip				
4.14	Homework/practice				
4.15	Note-taking				
4.16	Whole-class discussion				
4.17	Group class presentation				
4.18	Summary/reflection assignments				
4.19	Practicum/internship				

If there were other learning activities that were influential, please name them below.

Thank you for completing this questionnaire.

APPENDIX D

Original Learning Activities Survey (LAS)

This survey helps us learn about the experiences of adult learners. We believe that important things happen when adults learn new things. Only with your help can we learn more about this. The survey only takes a short time to complete, and your responses will be anonymous and confidential. Thank you for being part of this project; your cooperation is greatly appreciated.

1. Thinking about your educational experiences at this institution please check off any statements that may apply
    a. I had an experience that caused me to question the way I normally act.
    b. I had an experience that caused me to question my ideas about social roles. (Examples of social roles include what a mother or father should do or how an adult child should act.)
    c. As I questioned my ideas, I realized I no longer agreed with my previous beliefs or role expectations.
    d. Or instead, as I questioned my ideas, I realized I still agreed with my beliefs or role expectations.
    e. I realized that other people also questioned their beliefs.
    f. I thought about acting in a different way from my usual beliefs and roles.
    g. I felt uncomfortable with traditional social expectations.
    h. I tried out new roles so that I would become more comfortable or confident in them.
    i. I tried to figure out a way to adopt these new ways of acting.

j. I gathered the information I needed to adopt these new ways of acting.
k. I began to think about the reactions and feedback from my new behavior.
l. I took action and adopted these new ways of acting.
m. I do not identify with any of the statements above.

2. Since you have been taking courses at this institution, do you believe you have experienced a time when you realized that your values, beliefs, opinions or expectations had changed?

   Yes, if "Yes" please go to question #3 and continue the survey.

   No, if "No" please go to question #6 to continue the survey.

3. Briefly describe what happened?

4. Which of the following influenced this change? (Check all that apply)

   Was it a person who influenced the change ☐ Yes ☐ No
   ☐ Another student's support   ☐ A challenge from your teacher
   ☐ Your classmates' support   ☐ Your teacher's support
   ☐ Your advisor's support   ☐ Other _____

Was it a part of a class assignment that influenced the change?

   ☐ Yes   ☐ No

If "Yes," what was it? (Check all that apply)

   ☐ Class/group projects   ☐ Verbally discussing your concerns
   ☐ Writing about your concerns
   ☐ Personal journal   ☐ Term papers/essays
   ☐ Nontraditional structure of a   ☐ Self-evaluation in a course
     course   ☐ Class activity/ exercise
   ☐ Internship or co-op   ☐ Lab experiences
   ☐ Deep, concentrated thought   ☐ Personal reflection
   ☐ Personal learning assessment   ☐ Assigned readings
     (PLA)
   ☐ Other _____

Was it a significant change in your life that influenced the change?

   ☐ Yes   ☐ No

If "Yes," what was it? (Check all that apply)
- ☐ Marriage
- ☐ Birth/adoption of a child
- ☐ Moving
- ☐ Divorce/Separation
- ☐ Death of a loved one
- ☐ Change of job
- ☐ Loss of a job
- ☐ Retirement
- ☐ Other _____

5. Thinking back to when you first realized that your views or perspective had changed, what did your being in school have to do with the experience of change?

6. Would you characterize yourself as one who usually thinks back over previous decisions or past behavior?

☐ Yes   ☐ No

Would you say that you frequently reflect upon the meaning of your studies for yourself, personally?

☐ Yes   ☐ No

7. Which of the following have been part of your experience at this institution? (Please check all that apply.)
- ☐ Another student's support
- ☐ Your classmates' support
- ☐ Your advisor's support
- ☐ Class/group projects
- ☐ Writing about your concerns
- ☐ Personal journal
- ☐ Nontraditional structure of a course
- ☐ Internship or co-op
- ☐ Deep, concentrated thought
- ☐ Personal learning assessment (PLA)
- ☐ A challenge from your teacher
- ☐ Your teacher's support
- ☐ Verbally discussing your concerns
- ☐ Term papers/essays
- ☐ Self-evaluation in a course
- ☐ Class activity/exercise
- ☐ Lab experiences
- ☐ Personal reflection
- ☐ Assigned readings
- ☐ Other _____

Which of the following occurred while you have been taking courses at this institution?

- ☐ Marriage
- ☐ Birth/adoption of a child
- ☐ Moving
- ☐ Divorce/Separation
- ☐ Death of a loved one
- ☐ Change of job
- ☐ Loss of a job
- ☐ Retirement
- ☐ Other _____

8. Sex

    ☐ Male ☐ Female

9. Marital status

    - ☐ Single
    - ☐ Divorced/Separated
    - ☐ Married
    - ☐ Widowed
    - ☐ Partner

10. Race:

    - ☐ White, non-Hispanic
    - ☐ Asian or Pacific Islander
    - ☐ Other _____
    - ☐ Black, non-Hispanic
    - ☐ Hispanic

11. Current Major

    - ☐ Allied health
    - ☐ Business
    - ☐ Computer Science
    - ☐ General Arts/Liberal Studies
    - ☐ Other _____
    - ☐ Nursing
    - ☐ Science / Engineering
    - ☐ Social sciences (education, psychology, sociology)

12. Prior education:

    - ☐ High school diploma/GED
    - ☐ Associates degree
    - ☐ Bachelors degree
    - ☐ Masters degree
    - ☐ Doctorate
    - ☐ Other: _____

13. How many semesters have you been enrolled at this institution? _____

14. Age:

    - ☐ Below 21
    - ☐ 40–49
    - ☐ 21–24
    - ☐ 50–59
    - ☐ 25–29
    - ☐ 60–69
    - ☐ 30–39
    - ☐ Over 70

Thank you for completing this questionnaire.

Bibliography

"Abiy Ahmed Moves to Unite the Protestant Church in Ethiopia." Borkena, 20 June 2019. https://borkena.com/2019/06/20/ethiopia-protestant-churches-get-15-members-committee-to-unite/.

ACTEA. "Accredited Programs and Institutions," n.d. https://www.acteaweb.org/index.php/2014-05-24-01-24-56/programmes-and-institutions.

Akin, Daniel, ed. *Theology for the Church*. 2nd ed. Nashville, TN: Broadman & Holman, 2007.

Allison, Gregg R. "Humanity, Sin, and Christian Education." In *A Theology for Christian Education*, by James R. Estep, Michael J. Anthony, and Gregg R. Allison, 174–99. Nashville, TN: B & H Academic, 2008.

Anderson, Lorin W., David R. Krathwohl, Peter W. Airsasian, Kathleen A. Cruiskshank, Richard E. Mayer, Paul R. Pintrich, James Paths, and Merlin C. Wittrock, eds. *A Taxonomy for Learning, Teaching, and Assessing: A Revision of Bloom's Taxonomy of Educational Objectives*. New York: Longman, 2001.

Anderson, Valerie, and Suzanne Hidi. "Teaching Students to Summarize." *Educational Leadership* 46, no. 4 (1988/1989): 26–28.

Aron, Arthur, Elaine Arthur, and Elliot J. Coups. *Statistics for Psychology*. Upper Saddle River, NJ: Pearson Education, 2006.

Bain, Ken. *What the Best College Teachers Do*. Cambridge, MA: Harvard University Press, 2004.

Banks, Robert. *Reenvisioning Theological Education: Exploring a Missional Alternative to Current Models*. Grand Rapids: Eerdmans, 1999.

Barth, Roland S. *Learning by Heart*. San Francisco, CA: Jossey-Bass, 2001.

Bligh, D. A. *What's the Use of Lectures?* San Francisco, CA: Jossey-Bass, 2000.

Bloom, B., M. Englehart, D. Krathwohl, and W. Hill. *Taxonomy of Educational Objectives. Handbook I: Cognitive Domain*. London: Longmans, 1956.

Boyd, Robert D., and J. Gordon Myers. "Transformative Education." *International Journal of Lifelong Education* 7, no. 4 (1988): 261–84.

Brookfield, Stephen. *The Skillful Teacher: On Technique, Trust, and Responsiveness in the Classroom*. 2nd ed. San Francisco, CA: Jossey-Bass, 2006.

Bushnell, Horace. *Christian Nurture*. Grand Rapids: Baker Books, 1979.

Coley, Ken. *Teaching for Change: Eight Keys for Transformational Bible Study with Teens*. Nashville, TN: Randall House, 2016.

Coley, Kenneth S. "How Would It Play in Peoria?: Presenting Current Curriculum and Instruction Andragogy to Theological Educators in Santiago, Cuba." *Christian Education Journal* 12, no. 2 (2015): 415–29.

Coley, Kenneth S., and John Turner. "Examining Deuteronomy 6 Through the Lens of 21st Century Educational Concepts." *D6 Family Ministry Journal* 3 (May 1, 2018): 3–24.

Craig A. Mertler, and Rachel A. Vannatta. *Advanced and Multivariate Statistical Methods: Practical Application and Interpretation*. 3rd ed. California: Pyrczak Publishing, 2005.

Cranton, Patricia. *Understanding and Promoting Transformative Learning: A Guide for Educators of Adults*. 2nd ed. San Francisco, CA: Jossey-Bass, 2006.

Creswell, John W. *Research Design: Qualitative, Quantitative, and Mixed Methods Approaches*. 4th ed. Thousand Oaks: SAGE Publications, 2014.

Curzon, L. B. *Teaching in Further Education: An Outline of Principles and Practice*. New York, NY: Continuum, 2006.

Damasio, Antonio R. *Descartes' Error: Emotion, Reason, and the Human Brain*. New York: G. P. Putman's sons, 1994.

Das, Rupen. *Connecting Curriculum with Context: A Handbook for Context Relevant Curriculum Development in Theological Education*. Carlisle: Langham Global Library, 2015.

Davis, Barbara Gross. *Tools for Teaching*. 2nd ed. San Francisco, CA: Jossey-Bass, 2009.

Deininger, Fritz. "Foundations for Curriculum Design in Theological Education." In *Leadership in Theological Education*. Vol. 2, *Foundations for Curriculum Design*, edited by Fritz Deininger and Orbelina Eguizabal, 11–36. Carlisle: Langham Global Library, 2017.

Dirkx, John M., Jack Mezirow, and Patricia Cranton. "Musings and Reflections on the Meaning, Context, and Process of Transformative Learning: A Dialogue Between John M. Dirkx and Jack Mezirow." *Journal of Transformative Education* 4, no. 2 (April 2006): 123–39. https://doi.org/10.1177/1541344606287503.

Dosch, Mary, and Margaret Zidon. "'The Course Fits Us': Differentiated Instruction in the College Classroom." *International Journal of Teaching and Learning in Higher Education* 26, no. 3 (2013): 343–57.

Elmer, Muriel I., and Duane H. Elmer. *The Learning Cycle: Insights for Faithful Teaching from Neuroscience and the Social Sciences*. Downers Grove, IL: InterVarsity Press, 2020.

Ellington, Henry. *How Students Learn: A Review of Some of the Main Theories.* Aberdeen: Robert Gordon University, 1996.

Estep, James R., Michael J. Anthony, and Gregg R. Allison. *A Theology for Christian Education.* Nashville, TN: B & H Academic, 2008.

Ferris, Robert W., John R. Lillis, and Ralph E. Enlow, Jr. *Ministry Education that Transforms: Modeling and Teaching the Transformed Life.* Carlisle: Langham Global Library, 2018.

Festinger, Leon. *A Theory of Cognitive Dissonance.* Stanford: Stanford University Press, 1957.

Freire, Paulo. *Education for Critical Consciousness.* New York: Continuum, 2005.

———. *Pedagogy of the Oppressed.* London: Penguin Books, 1996.

Gay, L. R., Geoffrey E. Mills, and Peter W. Airasian. *Educational Research: Competencies for Analysis and Applications.* 8th ed. Upper Saddle River, NJ: Pearson Merrill Prentice Hall, 2006.

Gerke, Philip J. "Learning Experiences and Perspective Transformation in Evangelical Faith-Based Adult Nonformal Education Programs." PhD dissertation, University of Arkansas, 2013.

Gimple, Ryan K. "Integrating Transformative Learning Theory with Covenant Epistemology: An Exploration of the Missiological Implications." PhD dissertation, Southeastern Baptist Theological Seminary, 2018. ProQuest (AAT 10979248).

Graham, Donovan L. *Teaching Redemptively: Bringing Grace and Truth into Your Classroom.* 2nd ed. Colorado Springs, CO: Purposeful Design Publications, 2009.

Grudem, Wayne. *Systematic Theology: An Introduction to Biblical Doctrine.* Grand Rapids: Zondervan, 1994.

Harris, M. J., and R. Rosenthal. "Mediation and International Expectancy Effects: 31 Meta-Analysis." *Psychological Bulletin* 97, no. 3 (1985): 363–86. https://doi.org/10.1037/0033-2909.97.3.363

Harvey, P. H. B. "Transformative Learning in Undergraduate Education." *Dissertation Abstracts International* 65, no. 10 (2004), 3717A. (UMI No. NQ94535).

Henry, C. F. H. "Image of God." In *Evangelical Dictionary of Theology*, 2nd ed., edited by Walter A. Elwell, 591–94. Grand Rapids: Baker Academic, 2001.

Hoekema, Anthony A. *Created in God's Image.* Grand Rapids: Eerdmans Publishing, 1986.

Hoggan, Chad, Kaisu Mälkki, and Fergal Finnegan. "Developing the Theory of Perspective Transformation: Continuity, Intersubjectivity, and Emancipatory Praxis." *Adult Education Quarterly* 67, no. 1 (February 2017): 48–64, https://doi.org/10.1177/0741713616674076.

Hwang, I. "The Relationships between Discipleship Training and Transformative Learning in Korean Presbyterian Congregations." *Dissertation Abstracts International* 65, no. 5 (2004), 1625A. (UMII No. 31324775).

Issler, Klaus D., and Ronald T. Habermas. *How We Learn: A Christian Teacher's Guide to Educational Psychology*. Grand Rapids: Baker Books, 1994.

Keathley, Kenneth D., and Mark F. Rooker. *40 Questions About Creation and Evolution*. Grand Rapids: Kregel, 2014.

King, Kathleen P. "Examining Learning Activities and Transformational Learning," *International Journal of University Adult Education* 36, no. 3 (1997): 23–37.

———. *Handbook of the Evolving Research of Transformative Learning: Based on the Learning Activities Survey*. Charlotte, NC: Information Age Publishing, 2009.

Kolb, David A. *Experiential Learning: Experience as the Source of Learning and Development*. 2nd ed. Upper Saddle River, NJ: Pearson Education, 2015.

Lausanne Movement. "The Cape Town Commitment: A Confession of Faith and a Call to Action." Lausanne Movement, 2011. https://lausanne.org/content/ctcommitment#capetown.

LeBar, Lois. *Education That Is Christian*. Wheaton, IL: Victor Books, 1989.

Madsen, Susan R., and Bradley J. Cook. "Transformative Learning: UAE, Women, and Higher Education." *Journal of Global Responsibility* 1, no. 1 (2010): 127–48. doi.org/ 10.1108/20412561011039744. Retrieved 28 January 2021 from https://www.researchgate.net/publication/228387203_Transformative_learning_UAE_women_and_higher_education.

Mälkki, Kaisu. "Building on Mezirow's Theory of Transformative Learning: Theorizing the Challenges to Reflection." *Journal of Transformative Education* 8, no. 1 (2010): 42–62. https://doi.org/10.1177%2F1541344611403315.

———. "Theorizing the Nature of Reflection." PhD dissertation, University of Helsinki, Helsinki, 2011. https://helda.helsinki.fi/bitstream/handle/10138/26421/ theorizi.pdf?sequence=1.

Mandyk, Jason. *Operation World: The Definitive Prayer Guide to Every Nation*. 7th ed. Downers Grove, IL: InterVarsity Press, 2010.

Marzano, Robert J. *The Art and Science of Teaching: A Comprehensive Framework for Effective Instruction*. Alexandria, VA: Association for Supervision and Curriculum Development, 2007.

Marzano, Robert J., Jana S. Marzano, and Debra J. Pickering. *Classroom Instruction That Works: Research-Based Strategies for Every Teacher*. Alexandria, VA: Association for Supervision and Curriculum Development, 2003.

Mekonnen, Biadgelign A. *General Learning-Teaching Methods and Techniques*. Addis Ababa, Ethiopia: Addis Ababa Printing Press, 2010.

Merriam, Sharan B., Rosemary S. Caffarella, and Lisa Baumgartner. *Learning in Adulthood: A Comprehensive Guide*. 3rd ed. San Francisco, CA: Jossey-Bass, 2007.

Mezirow, Jack. "Epistemology of Transformative Learning." 2003. Accessed 12 July 2019. http://citeseerx.ist.psu.edu/viewdoc/download?doi=10.1.1.116.8014&rep=rep1&type=pdf.

———. *Transformative Dimensions of Adult Learning*. San Francisco, CA: Jossey-Bass, 1991.

———. "Transformative Learning: Theory to Practice." *New Direction for Adult and Continuing Education*, no. 74 (Summer 1997): 5–12. https://www.ecolas.eu/eng/wp-content/uploads/2015/10/Mezirow-Transformative-Learning.pdf

Mezirow, Jack, and Edward W. Taylor. *Transformative Learning in Practice: Insights from Community, Workplace, and Higher Education*. San Francisco, CA: Jossey-Bass, 2009.

Meserete Kristos College. "Who We Are." About Us, https://mkcollege.org/about-us-2/.

Mekane Yesus Seminary. n.d. www.eecmymys.edu.et.

Nacino-Brown, R., Festus E. Oke, and Desmond P. Brown. *Curriculum and Instruction: An Introduction to Methods of Teaching*. London: Macmillan, 1992.

Newton, Gary C. *Heart-Deep Teaching: Engaging Students for Transformed Lives*. Nashville, TN: B & H Academic, 2012.

Ott, Bernhard. *Understanding and Developing Theological Education*. Carlisle: Langham Global Library, 2016.

Pazmiño, Robert W. *Foundational Issues in Christian Education*. 2nd ed. Grand Rapids: Baker Books, 1997.

Polit, Denise F., and Bernadette P. Hungler. *Nursing Research: Principles and Methods*. 6th ed. Philadelphia: Lippincott, 1999.

Sanders, Paul. "Evangelical Theological Education in a Globalized World." Presentation given to the Centre for Theological Education, Belfast, Northern Ireland, 2009.

Shiloh Bible College Ethiopia. "Prospectus." https://docplayer.net/10830139-Shiloh-bible-college-ethiopia-prospectus.html.

Schunk, Dale H. *Learning Theories: An Educational Perspective*. 6th ed. Boston, MA: Pearson Education, 2012.

Shaw, Perry. "Holistic and Transformative: Beyond a Typology Approach to Theological Education." *Evangelical Review of Theology* 40, no. 3 (2016): 205–16.

———. *Transforming Theological Education: A Practical Handbook for Integrative Learning*. Carlisle: Langham Global Library, 2014.

Simpson, Elizabeth J. "The Classification of Educational Objectives, Psychomotor Domain." University of Illinois, Urbana, Illinois, 1966. https://files.eric.ed.gov/fulltext/ED010368.pdf.

Smith, James K. A. *Desiring the Kingdom: Worship, Worldview, and Cultural Formation*. Grand Rapids: Baker Academic, 2009.

Sousa, David A. *How the Brain Learns*. 5th ed. Thousand Oaks, CA: SAGE Publishing, 2017.

Stuckey, Heather L., Edward W. Taylor, and Patricia Cranton. "Developing a Survey of Transformative Learning Outcomes and Processes Based on Theoretical Principles." *Journal of Transformative Education* 11, no. 4 (October 2013): 211–28. https://doi.org/10.1177/1541344614540335.

Taylor, Edward W. "Transformative Learning Theory." *New Directions for Adult and Continuing Education*, no. 119 (Fall 2008): 5–15. https://doi.org/10.1002/ace.301.

———. "Transformative Learning Theory: A Neurobiological Perspective of the Role of Emotions and Unconscious Ways of Knowing." *International Journal of Lifelong Education* 20, no. 3 (June 2001): 218–36. https://doi.org/10.1080/02601370110036064.

Tomlinson, C. A. *The Differentiated Classroom: Responding to the Needs of All Learners*. Alexandria, VA: Association for Supervision and Curriculum Development, 1999.

Tomlinson, C. A., and Jay McTighe. *Integrating Differentiated Instruction and Understanding by Design: Connecting Content and Kids*. Alexandria, VA: Association for Supervision and Curriculum Development, 2006.

Tomlinson, C. A., and M. B. Imbeau. *Leading and Managing a Differentiated Classroom*. Alexandria, VA: Association for Supervision and Curriculum Development, 2010.

Tomlinson, C. A, and S. D. Allan. *Leadership for Differentiating Schools and Classrooms*. Alexandria, VA: Association for Supervision and Curriculum Development, 2000.

Vella, Jane. *Taking Learning to Task: Creative Strategies for Teaching Adults*. San Francisco, CA: Jossey-Bass, 2001.

Walberg, H. J. "Productive Teaching." In *New Directions for Teaching Practice and Research*, edited by H. C. Waxman and H. J. Walberg, 75–104. Berkeley, CA: McCutchen Publishing, 1999.

Wiggins, Grant, and Jay McTighe. *Understanding by Design*. 2nd ed. Alexandria, VA: Association for Supervision and Curriculum Development, 2005.

Wilson, Douglas. *Recovering the Lost Tools of Learning: An Approach to Distinctively Christian Education*. Wheaton, IL: Crossway, 1991.

Wubbels, T. "Interpersonal Relationships between Teachers and Students in the Classroom." In *New Directions for Teaching Practice and Research*, edited by H. C. Waxman and H. J. Walberg, 151–70. Berkeley, CA: McCutchen Publishing, 1999.

Yorks, L., and E. Kasl. "I Know More Than I Can Say: A Taxonomy for Using Expressive Ways of Knowing to Foster Transformative Learning." *Journal of Transformative Education* 4, no. 1 (2006): 43–64.

Zull, James E. *The Art of Changing the Brain: Enriching Teaching by Exploring the Biology of Learning.* Sterling, VA: Stylus, 2002.

Langham Literature, with its publishing work, is a ministry of Langham Partnership.

Langham Partnership is a global fellowship working in pursuit of the vision God entrusted to its founder John Stott –

> *to facilitate the growth of the church in maturity and Christ-likeness through raising the standards of biblical preaching and teaching.*

Our vision is to see churches in the Majority World equipped for mission and growing to maturity in Christ through the ministry of pastors and leaders who believe, teach and live by the word of God.

Our mission is to strengthen the ministry of the word of God through:
- nurturing national movements for biblical preaching
- fostering the creation and distribution of evangelical literature
- enhancing evangelical theological education

especially in countries where churches are under-resourced.

Our ministry

Langham Preaching partners with national leaders to nurture indigenous biblical preaching movements for pastors and lay preachers all around the world. With the support of a team of trainers from many countries, a multi-level programme of seminars provides practical training, and is followed by a programme for training local facilitators. Local preachers' groups and national and regional networks ensure continuity and ongoing development, seeking to build vigorous movements committed to Bible exposition.

Langham Literature provides Majority World preachers, scholars and seminary libraries with evangelical books and electronic resources through publishing and distribution, grants and discounts. The programme also fosters the creation of indigenous evangelical books in many languages, through writer's grants, strengthening local evangelical publishing houses, and investment in major regional literature projects, such as one volume Bible commentaries like the *Africa Bible Commentary* and the *South Asia Bible Commentary*.

Langham Scholars provides financial support for evangelical doctoral students from the Majority World so that, when they return home, they may train pastors and other Christian leaders with sound, biblical and theological teaching. This programme equips those who equip others. Langham Scholars also works in partnership with Majority World seminaries in strengthening evangelical theological education. A growing number of Langham Scholars study in high quality doctoral programmes in the Majority World itself. As well as teaching the next generation of pastors, graduated Langham Scholars exercise significant influence through their writing and leadership.

To learn more about Langham Partnership and the work we do visit **langham.org**

www.ingramcontent.com/pod-product-compliance
Lightning Source LLC
Chambersburg PA
CBHW070804230426
43665CB00017B/2488